For my grandmother,
who introduced me
to all things natural
and beautiful,
and my daughter,
a dedicated
salad eater.

To Una with lots of love
& a happy birthday 1994
& hoping you will have lots
of long days enjoying these
things.

THE SALAD BOOK

THE SAL

AD BOOK

CLARE CONNERY PHOTOGRAPHS BY CHRISTOPHER HILL

WEIDENFELD
AND
NICOLSON
LONDON

CONTENTS

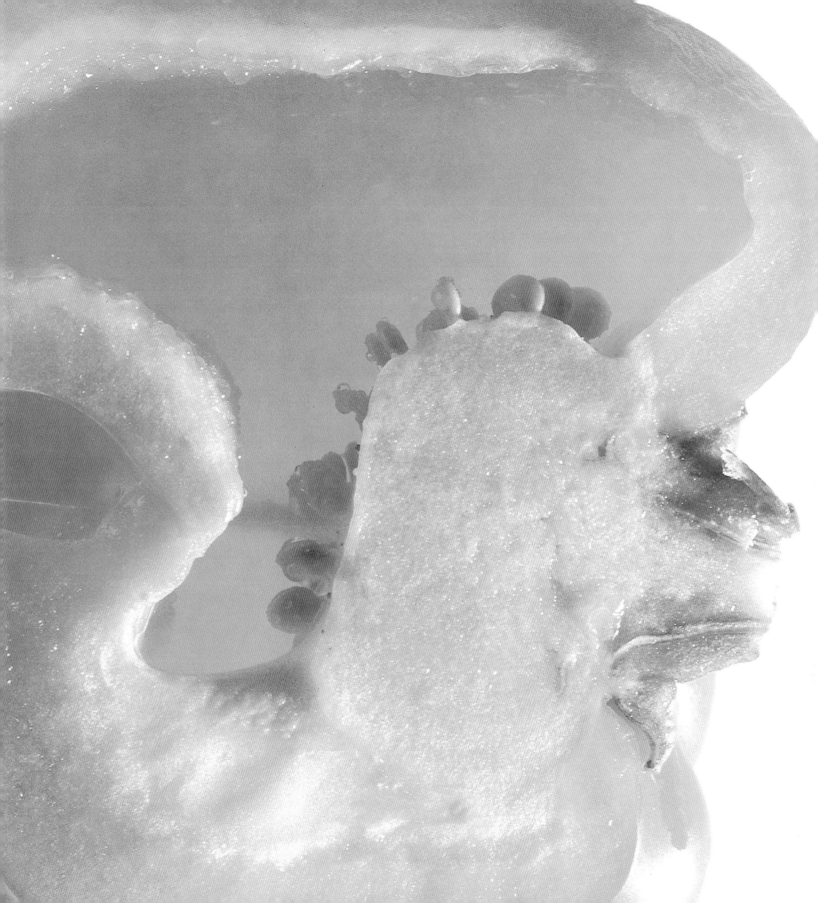

INTRODUCTION

Ever since the day I crouched in hiding between the tightly packed rows of garden peas in my grandmother's kitchen garden and picked my first illicit crisp green pod, my love affair with the edible garden began. Here on this tiny patch of land, my grandmother lovingly grew most of her food, introduced me to the joys of fresh natural produce and taught me the rudiments of self-sufficiency: how to prepare the soil, to dig and to plant, to harvest and to store. It was here that I planted the ubiquitous Irish potato, the mainstay of the nation, along with its compatriots, the onion and the leek. I learnt how to set rows of carrots, parsnips and turnips; to grow cauliflowers, courgettes (zucchini), artichokes and marrows (squash), to tie up beans and peas of all varieties; and to appreciate sorrel, spinach and chard, along with the many members of the cabbage family.

It was here, too, that I planted my first salad garden with leaves of all shapes, colours and sizes with what seemed to me then an enchanting array of names: lamb's leaves, oak leaves, rocket, cos, iceberg and round. Clumps of herbs – lemon balm, thyme, marjoram, oregano, sage and fennel – were intermingled among the salad leaves and the vegetables, decorating the borders and filling out the flowerbeds. There was a rosemary bush, a bay tree and several varieties of mint buried in enamel buckets. Edible flowers like nasturtiums, pot marigolds, violas and pansies contributed a kaleidoscope of colour.

The fruit garden, too, was equally rambling, and played an important role in family meals, along with the vegetables and salad plants. Fruit bushes jostled with the raspberry canes hanging their berry-laden branches towards the soil, where the ripening strawberries rested on mats of protective straw. In other corners of the garden there were apple trees, with both cooking and eating varieties, and a plum and a cherry tree.

These first simple experiences of food and gardening in County Down on the north-east coast of Ireland set me on my gardening trail: a bewitching journey of discovery which I have enjoyed immensely over the years, a journey that has taken me to many gardens and nurseries throughout the country in search of both the familiar and the unusual in both plant varieties and methods of growing. I have seen and been enchanted by cottage gardens reminiscent of my grandmother's with brightly coloured borders of edible and non-edible plants, flowers and salad leaves sprawling comfortably from one bed to another. Accordingly, the formal potager and herb gardens of manor and other grand houses mesmerized me with their enviable size and the variety and abundance of their produce, but undesirable maintenance burden. I have also been intrigued by the ingenuity and creative skills shown where space, although very limited, has been used to the full, with tubs, barrels, baskets, pots and boxes bringing a kitchen garden to a handkerchief-size patio, terrace or veranda.

Throughout my wanderings I have found an ever-increasing variety of vegetables, herbs and plants to extend and enhance my own kitchen garden and bring renewed interest and variety to my all-important salad table. My kitchen garden, like my grandmother's, is also in County Down. It is surrounded by farmland, sand dunes and sea, nestling peacefully in the shadow of the Mourne Mountains. It is a little garden, no more than 37 sq m (400 sq ft) and, even though it is still developing and about to be extended, throughout the year it provides me with fresh vegetables, fruit and salad leaves, along with herbs and flowers which are in patches all over the garden and awaiting the creation of a more compact and ordered home. Each season I add a bit more, alter the arrangement, and my enjoyment and larder increase together.

Here at my country cottage I have recreated the garden of my youth and filled it not only with memories and plants from the past but also with more recent discoveries. It is here where the scent of fresh flowers and herbs pervades my cottage that I create my salad and vegetable dishes. Many, like the fruits and vegetables themselves, come from my past; others have been influenced by my travels and the talented chefs I have had the good fortune to know over the years; but most are inspired by the latest leaf or shoot and the colourful patchwork of vegetables bursting from the soil in my rambling, informal garden.

As I am unable to bring you my garden in person, this book is intended as a source of inspiration and relaxation. Let the words and the pictures bring tranquillity and calm and lead you to trust your own intuition when it comes to creating your own personal salad garden and, of course, a very individual salad table.

Dundrum
August 1992

CHAPTER ONE

THE SALAD GARDEN

*G*rowing one's own vegetables and salad leaves is, of course, not a new phenomenon, nor is it confined to the realms of grand gardens and stately homes. My grandmother's tiny but well-organized cottage plot was arranged neatly in rows to get the maximum productivity from the minimum amount of space. Many another country household has also managed to survive over the years on the scrapings from a little strip of land, even in the poorest, most barren and desolate areas. Although not ideal, it is surprising what can be grown in a very limited space to supplement the shopping basket. Even town dwellers need not be limited by space constraints: keen gardeners can acquire an allotment on which to grow fruit and vegetables, and those who are really determined can have great success planting pots, tubs, barrels and window boxes.

The careful gardener will be
rewarded with an enormous range
of fresh salad leaves and
vegetables.

When I was creating my first salad garden as a child, with guidance and inspiration from my grandmother, neither of us was fully aware of the nutritional value and importance of the fresh natural produce which we grew so enthusiastically and ate with such relish. We knew instinctively that the roots, seeds, pods, fruits and leaves we nurtured made us feel good, but we didn't know why. Today, however, scientific study and research suggest that the precious qualities of health and vitality are a direct result of our diet and lifestyle. It is little wonder then that my grandmother enjoyed an active and healthy life almost entirely free from the ravages of age until she died peacefully at the age of ninety, and that I, too, have been blessed with good health and an abundance of vitality.

In the continuing search for a life free from pain, illness and disease, many people are now beginning to adopt an eating pattern based on the principles my grandmother and I followed quite naturally all those years ago; a diet where emphasis is placed on fresh fruit, vegetables and salad leaves, with the other natural unadulterated produce of the land playing a secondary role and used only as required.

As the demand for these health-giving foods increases, so too does the need for a greater variety of produce to enable the enthusiastic cook to prepare a wide range of stimulating and enticing dishes. As a result, supermarkets, greengrocers and markets are encouraged to buy, import and sell an increasingly varied, some might even say 'exotic', range of produce. In addition, nurseries and seed merchants are constantly extending their range to cope with the ever-increasing demand from inspired gardeners and cooks wanting to grow their own healthy ingredients.

The salad garden, whether large or small, can provide a range of produce for the kitchen and table, given a little thought, imagination, planning and a varying degree of hard work. Where space is particularly limited, a careful selection of the plants to be grown is essential if the maximum benefit is to be obtained from the area. In my cottage garden in County Down, which is no more than 18 sq m (200 sq ft), I plant what I need most, what I use

Barbara Pilcher's garden in County Down includes many examples of the kitchen garden, from formal potager to cottage-style beds.

most frequently and what I can produce better and more cheaply than buying locally. As a result I have ended up with a clump of artichokes, not just because they grow so handsomely, but because even when past their best for eating, the deep-purple flower heads can grace the table in a stylish, non-edible arrangement; gooseberry, blackcurrant and redcurrant bushes; a few raspberry canes lolling carelessly against the perimeter fence; and three crowns of rhubarb. Normally I also plant several rows of leeks, soup celery, carrots and a few drills of potatoes; however, this year I gave over their space entirely to a colourful and decorative range of salad leaves. I require a constant supply because I eat them so often, indeed at every meal. I will always make the space to grow my salad plants because I find that there are few areas in the garden where the reward for so little effort is so great in terms of variety, flavour, colour and freshness: qualities that can so rarely be bought. This year my planting was so successful that I had enough leaves to feed my family and my restaurant customers.

In May I prepared the soil and planted about ten different varieties of salad leaves, a very small number considering the vast range now available. Nonetheless, it was all I had space for. I selected them for their variety of colour, texture, taste and appearance. To be traditional, and in many ways quite ordinary, I planted the floppy round or butterhead variety (Boston lettuce); the iceberg, with its crisp, tightly packed head of pale green leaves; and the long-leaved cos with its rich green, oval leaves and crisp, pale heart. I then became more adventurous with the non-hearting lettuces, choosing the red and green 'Salad Bowl' variety with its pretty, indented leaves, rather like those of the oak leaf, and a more tightly packed variety called 'Warpath'; I also chose a green and a red 'Lollo' with their wonderfully frilly leaves and a more substantial big-hearted lettuce with red-tinged leaves called 'Marvel of Four Seasons', at its best in early summer, but also making an appearance in autumn. I also planted curly endive (frisée) with its frilly, deeply curled, long, narrow leaves, and a heavy supply of sorrel leaves to give a sharp lemony flavour to more bland leaves, as well as to soups, sauces and omelettes. Perhaps not a hugely inspiring or adventurous collection, but one which sparkles when complimented by a variety of herbs and edible flowers from the decorative borders.

My basic culinary herbs form a sprawling but attractive border around the edge of the vegetable beds, as well as decorative clumps in many of my flower beds. They include both broad and curly-leaf parsley, cress, thyme, sage, marjoram, oregano, mint, lemon balm, chives, tarragon, fennel, dill, chervil, borage and lovage. All in all it's a bit of a squeeze, but the results have been excellent and the effort most rewarding. With the acquisition of an additional piece of land, next year I will be able to grow both my vegetables and salad leaves in a much more orderly and controlled way and increase the number of varieties, as well as add more fruits, fruit bushes and trees.

My city garden, despite being about the same size as the country vegetable plot, has not always been easy to plant and maintain. Time is my constant enemy and it has taught me to be content with a small herb bed, and a few pots, tubs and barrels of lettuce plants to ensure that I am well fed during my days in the city. Perhaps one year I will enlist some help to get both areas running successfully.

*P*LANNING A SALAD GARDEN

The secret of planting a successful salad garden is to plan carefully and organize well within the limitations imposed by size, site and climate. Every garden is unique, making it a creative challenge for the gardener. The final design, however, will of course be determined by the amount of space available, the shape of that space, the type of salad vegetables to be planted and their individual growth requirements. The best results, however, are obtained in an open, but not exposed, position which gets plenty of sunlight. Where possible, the rows of plants should run north to south, making the maximum use of the available light.

Traditionally vegetables have been grown in long rows with an access path between each row. This, however, requires a considerable amount of space; today's premium land rates cut out the unproductive paths, enabling the

The author's cottage garden where a wide variety of salad leaves, including red and green 'Salad Bowl', curly endive (frisée) and cos, grow surrounded by herbs and fruit bushes.

amount of land available for crops to be doubled. As a result, the single rows can in many cases be turned into narrow strips or beds which are easily and efficiently worked from the surrounding paths.

THE SMALL GARDEN

If the garden is small and space is at a premium, plants need to be grown so as to ensure the maximum variety and yield. This is best achieved by planting the vegetables close together in blocks of deep beds of loose, organically-rich soil. This method of growing vegetables has been practised around the world for centuries and is known as the deep-bed method. It encourages the roots of the plants to grow downwards rather than spreading outwards, which not only gives a far heavier yield, but helps prevent weeds. The usual width of a deep bed is between 1–2 m (3–6 ft), which is both practical and efficient. It can be any length desired, with paths bordering the beds so that the plants can easily be reached and tended without treading on and compacting

the soil. The crops should be planted in blocks rather than rows, with the plants set out in a series of staggered lines forming a triangular pattern, where each plant is the same distance from those surrounding it. When the plants are mature, each will more or less just touch its neighbours.

Where space for a vegetable or even salad patch is practically non-existent, the 'cottage garden' design developed by 'cottagers' in England as a way of having both an ornamental and productive garden is ideal. Here, decorative and vegetable plants are grown in the same beds or borders, creating not only an attractive display but making the maximum use of available space. Small, colourful plants such as red chicory, the red, lettuce-like lollo rosso and the compact 'Marvel of Four Seasons' fit comfortably along the borders, while taller plants such as globe artichokes, climbing beans, miniature apple and pear trees, and the stately cordons can reside at the back, with ornamental cabbages, kale and ruby chard resting in the middle. Herbs, too, both small and large, can be incorporated in such beds as much for their scent, colour and appearance as for their culinary uses. An added benefit of the cottage garden is that the combination of flowers and salad leaves attracts useful insects and pest predators, keeping both the edible and decorative crops in peak condition. It is worth noting, however, that plenty of compost needs to be dug into the areas where the salad plants are to be grown, as they require a more fertile soil than the ornamental plants.

THE FORMAL KITCHEN GARDEN

Where space is not a problem, and time and talent are in abundance, a formally laid out and decorative kitchen garden, such as the French kitchen gardens or potagers of the sixteenth and seventeenth centuries, can be created. In these gardens vegetables were arranged in patterns in formal beds just like the flowers and shrubs in a formal flower or herb garden. The best example of a reconstructed

LEFT Decorative plants, vegetables and salad leaves growing in a mixed border make the maximum use of space.
FAR LEFT A section of the Royal Horticultural Society's model garden at Wisley. FOLLOWING PAGE Rosemary Verey's potager at Barnsley House in Gloucestershire.

15

Renaissance potager is at Château Villandry in the Loire Valley in France, where square beds are arranged in a symmetrical design with the different varieties of salad plants planted so as to create solid blocks of colour.

In England in the mid 1970s, Rosemary Verey, a renowned plantswoman and gardening writer, began work on a potager in the grounds of Barnsley House, her home in Gloucestershire. Today it is one of Britain's finest examples of a traditional potager. The layout, based on a seventeenth-century design, is essentially rectangular in shape, two thirds of the area being divided into four squares by brickwork paths united by a central focal point. The remaining area is divided in half by a decorative tunnel. Within each of the principal square beds, which range in width from about 60 cm to 1.5 m (2–5 ft), a variety of vegetables and herbs are planted in different geometric patterns carefully grouped so that their colour and ornamental qualities are displayed to the full.

Not far from my cottage in Northern Ireland, botanist Barbara Pilcher has also created a potager in her country garden. Although much smaller than Rosemary Verey's, it is also divided into squares, based on a geometric design with a central focal point, brick paths and herb hedges. It shows what can be achieved within a limited area.

In addition to the potager Barbara Pilcher's garden also has examples of the other main styles of kitchen garden;

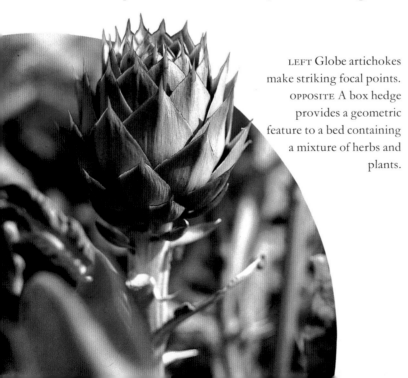

LEFT Globe artichokes make striking focal points. OPPOSITE A box hedge provides a geometric feature to a bed containing a mixture of herbs and plants.

from the long, narrow rows of the conventional garden to the deep block beds of the space-saving plot, as well as wild and rambling cottage beds and borders and a variety of tubs, pots, urns and containers arranged around the house and outbuildings. It is a kitchen gardener's paradise and has been an inspiration to me and many others over the years, particularly before I had the time to develop my own separate vegetable, salad and herb areas.

When such beautiful, decorative and practical kitchen gardens are both being designed or in the process of evolving, it is not only the basic shape or structure of the beds which is important, but also the type of plants, their position and other details, such as focal points and hedges, borders and paths. As I have already mentioned, the choice of which salad vegetables and leaves to grow depends on individual requirements, but where space is available, a few 'feature' plants can be included to give depth and interest to the overall arrangement. I have included a few of these in my own simple garden, and they are stunning additions. One of the most handsome of all vegetables is the cardoon. With its thistle-like leaves and heads, and grey foliage, it makes a magnificent focal point in a central position or a stunning backdrop for other plants. Lovage, angelica and the globe artichoke, also tall, handsome, leafy plants, can be used in exactly the same way, with equal success.

Fennel and sweet cicely, with their fine, fern-like foliage, also create delicate patches of texture in the salad garden, as long as they are kept under control and positioned tactfully, preferably along the boundary of the plot. Canes, too, can be positioned in such a way as to allow climbing vegetables like runner or French beans and cucumbers to enjoy a space in the garden without overrunning the more compact salad heads. Growing vegetables in this way, among the leaves, creates height and pattern throughout the plot.

Where a special feature is possible, an individual bed, whether round, triangular, oblong, square or hexagonal, indeed whatever shape is appropriate, can be designed to contain an interesting selection of plants with variety in colour, and contrast in texture and form.

To contain or finish the edges of the salad garden, small, neat hedges of box or herbs, such as bay, rosemary, parsley and chives, can be cultivated or clumps of various herbs used to create a less formal, yet equally satisfying arrange-

ment. The fluffy lettuces like Italian 'Lollo' in both red and green make a striking border, as do the edible flowers, pansies, pot marigolds and nasturtiums, which make a colourful addition to the salad bowl as well.

Between the beds and in many cases alongside them, paths for walking on and working from are not only very necessary and practical, but can also serve as a decorative feature. In the past I have built paths using discarded blocks from an obsolete storage heater, old weathered bricks from an ancient wall, small concrete slabs, and pieces put together like crazy paving, as well as a variety of local stones butted together. Many interesting patterns can be created with different arrangements.

THE CONTAINER GARDEN

Where space is so limited that thoughts of decorative borders, focal points and designer pathways seem altogether too esoteric, it is worth considering that small can also be beautiful and that stunning and productive arrangements can be created with a little thought and careful choice of plants and containers. For example, a window box, tub or wheelbarrow make excellent planters or, if space is more restricted, a few plants can sit on a window sill, or indeed in any container available.

When growing a kitchen garden in containers of any variety, it is best to choose plants which are small, shallow-rooting and fast-growing. Vegetables such as tomatoes, cucumbers and peppers grow well in the restricted surroundings of a container, but when space is limited and variety is required, it is best to be content with the more productive and less demanding salad plants like the different lettuce varieties, sun-loving herbs like basil, thyme, marjoram, parsley and chives, or edible flowers like nasturtiums, pot marigolds and pansies. Miniature apple, plum and pear trees also grow well in containers, as do standard-size gooseberry and redcurrant bushes. Strawberries also make excellent tub and container plants and are extremely pretty. Shallow-rooting plants like onions, shallots, lettuce, spinach, rocket, purslane and herbs require a soil depth of about 10–15 cm (4–6 in) and can grow happily in small containers, such as flowerpots, tubs, old sinks, tin cans and even hanging baskets. Larger plants like tomatoes

and peppers need a soil depth of about 23–25 cm (9–10 in) and a much larger container like a grow bag, a wooden barrel or some other container, that is at least as wide as it is deep.

Provided the container is an appropriate size and the soil or potting compost is of good quality, there is no reason why containerized plants should not grow as well as those planted in the garden. If the container is to sit outside, it is best not to choose a peat-based compost as it dries out

ABOVE AND OPPOSITE Pots, urns and other containers can be filled with decorative plants, herbs, flowers and salad leaves to suit both the surroundings and individual tastes.

quickly and is difficult to re-hydrate. A soil-based compost, using a good quality top soil mixed with some well-rotted garden compost, is a good combination. To ensure that the soil drainage is good and prevent waterlogging, it is essential to make several holes in the bottom of the container to let excess water drain away. Alternatively, holes can be made about 2.5 cm (1 in) above the base of the container. This prevents the container from having to stand on blocks to keep it free-draining. In addition, before filling the container with soil, cover the drainage holes with pieces of broken pots laid concave-side down, and cover these with a little gravel, then a layer of coarse fibrous material such as turf, old sacking or dried leaves. This will prevent the compost from blocking the drainage holes.

Only very heavy rainfall will provide enough water to keep a container moist. It is therefore essential to water containerized plants regularly. In summer they will need to be watered every day. Wooden containers and hanging baskets can be lined with plastic to help retain water, but they, too, need a few holes punched in their fabric to facilitate drainage.

Plants in containers also require regular feeding because

ABOVE Herbs combine well in containers with colourful annuals such as lobelia. RIGHT Where space is more limited, herbs can easily be grown on a windowsill.

the nutrients are continually washed through the compost. This should be done weekly during the growing season using a liquid seaweed or animal manure.

Planting the Salad Garden

Whether the salad garden is developed in a container, a large pot or a flowerbed, the principles for growing a successful crop remain the same: a rich, well-drained soil,

which is frequently watered and fed during the growing season and protected from the elements in exposed areas. Where the soil is light and drains easily, it needs to have peat and well-made compost worked into it to increase its ability to hold water and consequently retain nutrients. Light soil, which heats up quickly, produces an excellent early salad crop but needs careful attention in the summer if the optimum yield is to be obtained. Heavier soils, in contrast, need to have plenty of bulky organic matter such as strawy manure worked into them to improve their drainage and help aerate the soil.

Although all vegetables have specific soil and mineral requirements, it is not always possible to satisfy these fully, as most of us have to make do with the soil type we have, feeding and manuring it to the best of our ability. Nonetheless, by grouping plants which have the same fundamental soil requirements, such as those belonging to the same botanical family or near relatives, and rotating them annually, the garden's limited resources can be used to the full and the soil given the chance to replenish its lost minerals and remain free from pests and disease.

The best way to do this is to divide the vegetable garden into three or four plots and to plant a different crop group in each plot every year over a three- or four-year cycle.

The main groups for rotation are the brassicas (which includes all members of the cabbage family, chinese cabbage, mustard greens, Brussels sprouts, cauliflower, calabrese, broccoli, kale, turnips, swedes [rutabagas], radishes and kohl-rabi); legumes (all peas and beans, including broad beans, runner beans, French beans, lima beans, soya beans, sweetcorn and okra, spinach, spinach beet, Swiss chard, chicory, endive, lettuce and cress); and root crops (including potatoes, carrots, parsnips, onions, shallots, leeks, garlic, tomatoes, courgettes [zucchini], marrows [squash], pumpkins, celery, Florence fennel, aubergines [eggplants], peppers, cucumbers, melons, celeriac, salsify and parsley).

Another bed or area should be left for the permanent

In this practical and well-ordered garden, each vegetable has been planted in a separate area. The paths not only provide ready access to the beds, but also serve as a decorative feature.

crops, such as globe artichokes, Jerusalem artichokes, asparagus, sea kale and herbs.

The vegetable-growing season begins either with the sowing of seeds, or the planting of mature seedlings directly into the ground. The seeds can also be planted indoors in pots or trays and transferred outdoors when the developed seedlings have been 'hardened off'. Seeds can be obtained from existing plants or bought from the garden centre or seedsmen's catalogues. Plants, ready for planting out, can also be bought from the nursery or garden centre, which is useful when time and space are limited. The disadvantage of buying ready-grown plants, however, is that selection is usually limited to the more common plants, like round lettuce, cauliflower and cabbages.

Outdoor sowing of seeds is suitable for robust vegetables which germinate easily, for crops which are sown thickly and harvested young, and for hardy crops like peas, beans and vegetables that do not like being transplanted.

Early crops are best sown indoors to begin with, either on a windowsill, in a greenhouse or in a propagator. This protects them from unfavourable weather conditions and enables them to become well established before being transferred outdoors. Raising plants indoors involves several different stages before planting in the open ground; sowing, pricking out, potting on and hardening off.

Sowing involves the planting of seeds in small containers or seed trays filled with a good quality, seed-sowing compost which is sterile, weed and disease free, and which retains water. Garden compost is not suitable as it is too rich for the germinating seeds and produces unhealthy, leggy and weak plants. The compost should come to within 12 mm ($\frac{1}{2}$ in) of the top of the tray or container and be well soaked but not waterlogged before planting. Sow the seeds thinly on the top of the compost, about 12–25 mm ($\frac{1}{2}$–1 in) apart, then sprinkle a little fine dry compost on top.

Seeds can also be sown in seed blocks: small sections of compressed potting compost with no more than one or two seeds to a block. This provides the seed with its own individual container and makes planting on much easier. The individual blocks are packed tightly into seed trays for convenience in handling. Sowing seeds in these blocks eliminates the need to prick out and enables each seedling to be planted directly into the prepared ground.

After sowing, the seed blocks are left to germinate in a warm place like an airing or kitchen cupboard, or above, but not directly on, a radiator or in a propagator, away from direct sunlight. When the seedling has two or three leaves, it is sturdy enough to handle. The block can now be carefully eased out of the seed tray and transferred to a slightly larger seed tray, also filled with moist potting compost. Holes should be made about 4 cm (1$\frac{1}{2}$ in) apart and large enough to accommodate the seedling's roots; its lower leaves should be just above the soil. The seed tray is then returned to its warm place.

When the plants have developed a strong root system, they can be transferred once again to a larger container or pot holding standard potting compost and, eventually, planted outdoors. Prior to this final transition, it is necessary to 'harden off' the plants so that the transfer to the outside world is not too big a shock. This is done by gradually introducing them to the light and air over a two to three week period: first in a well-lit and ventilated place indoors, then to a sheltered place outside, finally leaving the plants out day and night before planting them in the ground. Hardy plants, like most of the salad plants, can be planted out directly from the seed tray if weather conditions are favourable.

In temperate climates, the earliest crops of vegetables have to be grown in a heated greenhouse, but both the sowing and harvesting times can be brought forward by at least a month by using cloches. These simple protective covers are made from glass, plastic, fibreglass and polythene film and can form as substantial and rigid a structure as the material will allow or the plant requires. Shapes range from the low 'tent-shaped' cloches suitable only for small, low-growing plants like the salad varieties, to much taller cloches which can cover and protect bigger plants like tomatoes. They can be used over single plants or stretched over whole beds and, with the exception of those made from glass, are light and extremely mobile.

Garden frames, a form of miniature greenhouse, are also particularly useful for bringing on seeds, protecting young plants and hardening off others. Like the cloches, they are very useful throughout the year.

SPROUTED SEEDS

Seeds, however, do not always need protection from the elements, nor should one have to wait until they are full-sized plants to enjoy them. Seeds which are germinated in trays without soil and lightly watered will, in a few days' time, form small, tender shoots or sprouts, which are delicious to eat as well as being highly nutritious. Seed sprouting has been practised by many different peoples for over 5,000 years and is a highly intensive form of food production. Depending on the sprout species chosen, a crop will be ready for harvesting in two to five days or when the sprouts are between 6–12 mm ($\frac{1}{4}$–$\frac{1}{2}$ in) long. In the germination process, the fats and starches stored in the seed are converted into vitamins, minerals, proteins and sugars which are readily digested by our bodies and are therefore incredibly valuable foods when freshly harvested. Because they grow so quickly, they are at their best only briefly. It is therefore advisable to sprout small quantities at regular intervals to ensure a constant supply.

There are many different ways of sprouting seeds: in glass jars, bowls, dishes, plastic boxes, seed trays or in one of the many patented sprouters on the market. To find which method is best for you is really a matter of experimenting. My own preference is for a commercial sprouter which, being purpose built, is the most convenient to use.

Sprouted seeds (from left to right):
azuki, mung and alfalfa.

However, when I need large quantities of sprouts I use a raised seed tray with drainage holes lined with nylon mesh, which I prop over a bottom tray so that the water drains away easily. This prevents the seeds from becoming waterlogged and rotting.

The main principles to remember when sprouting seeds are to sow them no more than 1 cm ($\frac{1}{2}$ in) deep so that they will have room to expand to about four times their volume; to soak them overnight in cold water before sowing; to rinse them in cold water morning and evening; to ensure that they have good drainage; to grow them in a warm place either in the dark or in the light, depending on whether crisp, light-coloured sprouts or soft, green sprouts are required; and to harvest them when young and tender.

The amount of seeds harvested will obviously depend on the size of the sprouting container. Put one or two handfuls of seeds into a sieve and rinse under cold water before transferring them to a bowl with cold water and leaving to soak overnight. This allows the seeds to swell and accelerates the sprouting process. After soaking, rinse the seeds again before spreading them in the chosen container. Next put them in a warm place like an airing cupboard or on a sunny windowsill. The temperature should be between 13°C and 24°C (55°F and 70°F) to allow the seeds to germinate. The faster they germinate, the less likely they are to invite disease. They require rinsing in cold water twice a day, morning and evening. Rinsing is easier in patented sprouters which are designed so that water can be poured in and out of the container without removing the seeds. If a glass jar is used, muslin needs to be secured over the top and the water poured in and out through it. In my experience this method is the least successful way of both growing and watering sprouts as the muslin tends to get clogged and the seeds often rot due to insufficient drainage.

Depending on the type of seed grown, the sprouts will be ready for harvesting in two to three days. (See Sprouting Chart opposite.) Before using or storing the sprouts, rinse once more under cold running water, then drain. The sprouted seeds will keep for several days in a plastic bag or container in the refrigerator. Sometimes I even put

Alfalfa sprouted in a shallow glass dish. These four-day-old sprouts are now ready for use.

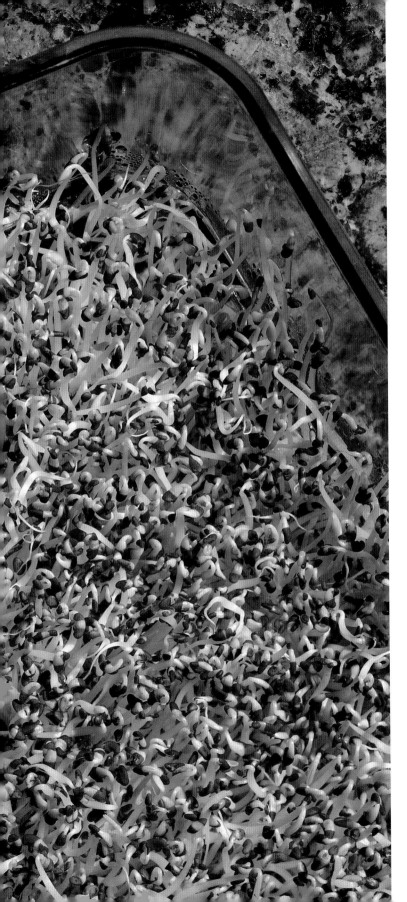

the seed tray into the fridge once the sprouts have reached their optimum size, which helps to extend their life.

Although sprouts are a storehouse of nutritional goodness, particularly when eaten raw, some, like red kidney beans, tomato seeds and seed potatoes, should not be sprouted at all as they are poisonous. The seeds given in the Sprouting Chart can all be grown and used raw or cooked.

SEEDS SUITABLE FOR SPROUTING

NAME	TASTE	AVERAGE TIME DAYS	LENGTH OF SPROUT
SMALL SEEDS:			
Alfalfa	Crisp refreshing taste	3–4	2.5–5 cm (1–2 in)
Fenugreek	Strong curry taste	3–4	1 cm ($\frac{1}{2}$ in)
Radish	Tastes just like radishes	3–5	1–2.5 cm ($\frac{1}{2}$–1 in)
LARGER SEEDS:			
Lentil	Dry lentil taste	3–5	5 mm–2.5 cm ($\frac{1}{4}$–1 in)
Azuki beans	A nutty taste	3–5	1–2.5 cm ($\frac{1}{2}$–1 in)
Mung	Crisp fresh taste	2–6	1–6 cm ($\frac{1}{2}$–2$\frac{1}{2}$ in)
Chick peas: soak for 18 hours and change water twice	Strong nutty taste	4–5	1 cm ($\frac{1}{2}$ in)
GRAINS:			
Wheat	Sweet taste	4–5	1–1.5 cm ($\frac{3}{4}$–1 in)
Rye	A distinct sweet taste	3–5	2.5–5 cm (1–2 in)
Barley	Sweet taste	3–5	1 cm ($\frac{1}{2}$ in)

Whether your kitchen garden is confined to a sprouting tray, glass jar or window box, or extended to a plot of ground, there is no reason why it should not be decorative as well as practical. Indeed, it should be as pleasing to the eye as it is to the palate.

29

CHAPTER TWO

PLANT PORTRAITS

*T*he colourful, exciting and wide range of salad leaves, vegetables, flowers and herbs grown in gardens and flowerbeds, in barrels and tubs on patios, and in pots and boxes on windowsills, provides the perfect raw material for the imaginative cook to produce a nutritious and unending variety of edible creations.

Many of these crops, like the soft, floppy butterhead lettuce, the cucumber, tomato and onion, have been used for years. Others, like the pretty Italian 'Lollo Rosso', fennel, courgette (zucchini), peppers, herbs and flowers, have been confined for years to the kitchens of the more adventurous and enlightened.

However, with an ever-increasing awareness and interest in natural, unadulterated food, salad ingredients of all types are being used throughout the menu from beginning to end. These salad ingredients can be divided into four different groups: salad leaves, salad vegetables, herbs and edible flowers, with each group's possibilities as varied and exciting as the cook-gardener desires.

Runner beans and violets not only
look decorative in the garden, but
also make wonderful salad
ingredients.

SALAD LEAVES

Salad leaves or leafy salad plants are perhaps the most rewarding salad crops to grow, not only because they grow quickly and look so attractive, but also because their flavour and texture always taste better than anything one can buy, and the variety is generally much greater and more colourful than that available in the local market.

Salad leaves, like the salad plants themselves, can be separated into a number of different groups: 'lettuce leaves', 'other leaves', and the family of 'brassicas' or 'cabbage'.

LETTUCE LEAVES

THE CABBAGE HEAD grouping includes the 'round heart' or 'butterhead' (Boston) lettuce, which has loose soft-textured leaves on the outside, with a tightly packed heart in the centre, similar to the cabbage itself, but with more delicate leaves and a slightly bland, sweet flavour. Two easily-grown varieties for the kitchen garden are 'Tom Thumb' and 'Trocadero'. Crisphead or cabbage-head lettuce is also included in this group. Its head is larger and more tightly packed than the butterhead variety and it has a crisper, more interesting texture. Although somewhat bland in flavour, crisphead lettuce remains crisp longer and makes an excellent base for other leaves. Good examples are 'Webb's Wonderful' and the American 'Iceberg'.

THE LONG-LEAF variety of lettuce is characterized by elongated heads of thick, crisp, textured, green, oval leaves and a pale green heart. 'Cos' or 'romaine' lettuce belongs to this category. Cos is thought to be the original name given to this lettuce by the Romans, who are believed to have discovered it on the Greek island of Cos. However, when the Romans eventually brought it to Europe, it became known as romaine, after those who brought it. Like iceberg lettuce, it has the ability to remain crisp although its more pungent flavour and interesting texture differentiate it from the cabbage-head variety. Cos lettuce takes longer to mature than other types of lettuce, but it can withstand hot, dry conditions better without going to seed. A popular variety of cos lettuce is 'Lobjoit's Green'. The small variety of lettuce called 'Little Gem', which is very crisp and sweet,

is a type of cos lettuce, but is much smaller and more compact.

THE LOOSE-LEAF variety, perhaps the largest group within the lettuce family, embraces all the lettuces which do not have particularly obvious heads. They are often referred to as 'gathering' or 'cutting' lettuce because the leaves can be individually picked as required, or the entire head cut off 2.5 cm (1 in) above the stem. In both cases the lettuce will grow again, hence its other name, 'cut and come again' lettuce. It is also referred to as 'Salad Bowl' lettuce. Its colour can vary from pale to dark green and from pinky red

ABOVE 'Salad Bowl' lettuce OPPOSITE Cabbage-head lettuce

'Marvel of Four Seasons'

Red and green chicories

to dark brown. Its leaves can also vary from the large and gently rounded 'Marvel of Four Seasons', to the curly and ruffled 'Lollo' varieties, as well as the deeply indented oak-leaf varieties. Loose-leaf lettuce is slower to run to seed than other types of lettuce. It is hardy and therefore useful over a long period.

OTHER LEAVES

This group includes members of the chicory and endive family, various salad greens and edible wild leaves. The largest single group of these is the chicory family.

CHICORY has dozens of different varieties, some used solely for their leaves, others for their roots. To confuse things even more, the name varies from country to country. The French and Americans call it endive, the British chicory, and the Belgians 'Witloof' (white leaf). Chicory leaves are a particularly attractive addition to the salad bowl

because of the wide variety of their colours, which range from the bright green of the 'Sugar Loaf' type to the rich ruby red of the Italian chicories and the variegated types. The most popular red varieties are 'Red Verona', 'Flanba', 'Tallarosa', 'Red Treviso' and 'Variegated Castelfranco'. The 'Sugar Loaf' and the Italian 'Grumolo' chicories are the most popular green varieties. They are generally available throughout the year, but are most valued for use in winter salads when the more delicate varieties of salad leaves are not so readily available.

'WITLOOF' CHICORY, also known as Belgian chicory, grows from the root of the chicory plant which is initially cultivated outdoors, then transplanted, forced and blanched in total darkness. This method produces a compact, conical head of crisp, white-yellow leaves about 13–25 cm (5–6 in) long, known as 'chicons'. Chicory has a pleasantly bitter and refreshing flavour which becomes stronger and less pleasant as it grows and ages. The colour, too, initially white tinged with lemon, becomes greener with age and exposure to light. It combines well with bland, delicate leaves.

ENDIVES are also members of the chicory family. The curly-leaved variety, *chicory frisée*, is a native of southern Asia and northern China. It has a low-growing head of large, curly, frilly-edged or indented leaves which range in colour from a rich deep green on the outside to a tightly packed centre of pale lemony green tendrils. The broad-leaved variety 'Batavian' endive, also known as *escarole*, *scarole* or *chicorée scarole*, is much taller and broader. It tends to be more hardy than the curly-leaved variety and is therefore more suitable for autumn and winter rather than spring and summer. Both varieties tend to have a slightly bitter flavour and are sometimes blanched to make them more delicate.

ROCKET, sometimes called Italian cress, roquette or rugula, is more correctly known as arugula. It grows wild throughout the Mediterranean countries and is particularly popular in France and southern Italy where it is an essential ingredient of *mesclun*, the Provençal mixture of small salad greens. The leaves have a fiery, spicy, slightly peppery flavour which combines well with milder plants. It should be eaten young when its smooth, notched, green leaves are small and delicate, and certainly before the plant flowers, when its leaves turn tough and bitter. It grows best in cool weather, tending to turn to seed quickly in summer. Its small cream flowers are also pretty in salads and for garnishes.

DANDELION is well known as a garden weed, being particularly prolific in some lawns. Although despised by many a gardener, its long, deeply notched leaves with their tart, astringent butteriness are highly prized by salad cooks, particularly in France and Italy where they are grown commercially. They were so highly regarded in Britain during Elizabethan times that the vegetable gardens of all great houses grew them. The bitter flavour is subtly changed by blanching, as with chicory, and the leaves, roots and flowers are used in salads. Dandelion leaves are at their

Curly-leaved endive (frisée)

best in the spring when they are young and pale green in colour. After June they tend to become coarse and bitter.

LAMB'S LETTUCE, also known as corn salad and *mâche*, was a wild plant long before it was cultivated. Its small, round, deep-green, velvety leaves commonly appear in meadows and through the stubble in cornfields all over Europe. It has a mild, refreshing flavour and is a pretty addition to any salad. It should be harvested when small and tender before flowering, either as a complete plant or as outer leaves only. This allows the plant to regenerate new growth. It is a hardy little plant and for this reason is most useful for winter and spring salads when its delicately flavoured leaves are at their best.

ABOVE Summer purslane
LEFT Lamb's lettuce
RIGHT Winter purslane

SUMMER PURSLANE has been cultivated in India and the Middle East for years and was also popular in Europe during the sixteenth century. Forms of purslane also grow wild in much of the temperate world. There are several varieties of this half-hardy annual which grow to a height of 15 cm (6 in). Some are more robust than others but all have a refreshing, crunchy texture despite a rather bland flavour. The fleshy green or golden leaves of summer purslane are small and spoon-like and grow in a rosette shape from a fat juicy stem. Both leaves and stems are edible and combine well with hotter-flavoured leaves and herbs.

WINTER PURSLANE is also known as claytonia or miner's lettuce. This hardy annual makes an excellent winter salad plant, providing several crops using the 'cut-and-come-again' principle. During the spring it grows very rapidly, producing narrow triangular leaves on short stalks. As it gets older, its stalks become longer, its leaves more rounded and wrapped around the stem. In spring it also produces pretty, edible, white flowers and is an indispensable plant for winter and early spring salads.

SPINACH leaves are highly nutritious and, when young and tender, are delicious in salads. Spinach and chard, the latter also known as silver beet, sea kale beet, leaf beet or Swiss chard, are very similar leafy vegetables. True spinach, however, is considered more delicate and refined in both appearance and flavour. It has smoother, paler leaves and does not grow as tall or as vigorously. It has a pleasant acidic taste due to the presence of oxalic acid. The chards have glossy, dark green leaves and an entirely different flavour to the spinach plant. Only the types known as spinach beet, perpetual spinach or cutting chard are used in salads. The leaves of the other varieties, although handsome, are coarse, thick-stemmed and best for cooking. Spinach beet produces a succession of fresh leaves over a long period, turning to seed only during its second year. It is the easiest to grow of all spinach crops.

Sorrel

SORREL is a very hardy perennial plant often found growing wild in an acid soil. The garden or common sorrel has narrow, spear-shaped leaves rather like small dock leaves, while Buckler leaf or French sorrel has shield-shaped leaves which are wider at their base. It is one of the first green plants to appear in spring rising above the grass. It is sometimes called dock and sourgrass because of its sharp, astringent flavour much enjoyed by farmworkers who chew it to quench their thirst while bringing in the hay. Buckler leaf or French sorrel is said to have a milder, more lemony flavour than the common or garden sorrel. Only a few leaves are required in a salad to give it an interesting, sharp flavour.

GOOD KING HENRY is an old-fashioned hardy perennial plant which has been known since neolithic times and was popular up until the last century. It is very similar in taste to spinach and sorrel and the young green leaves and flowering shoots can be used in salads. In recent years, due to the enthusiasm of salad gardeners, it has begun to make a comeback.

CRESSES

In addition to this wide variety of large salad leaves, there are also many small salad plants with tiny leaves, which not only look attractive, but also add a pungent, spicy flavour to the salad bowl, combining well with milder leaves. One group that has been cultivated for a long time, specifically for use in salads, is cress; indeed, it is often the first seed we grow – as children – mixed with mustard seed on wet blotting paper. It is widely sold in shops in small plastic boxes as mustard and cress, although it is more likely to be salad rape, a much milder-flavoured seed, but also a valued salad plant. The true cress, garden cress, is a more hot-flavoured plant which originated in western Asia, but now grows wild in many parts of the northern hemisphere and can easily be grown in a shallow layer of soil either indoors or outdoors, or on blotting paper, cotton wool, flannel, or in jars (see sprouting seeds p. 27). It quickly grows into a thick carpet of green leaves which can be cut many times, giving several crops in one season.

LANDCRESS is a hardy annual plant, also known as American or winter cress. It provides peppery-flavoured leaves all year round and will thrive well in a damp, shady area of the garden. After sowing, it will provide aromatic, bright-green clusters of serrated leaves in about eight weeks. The outer leaves should be picked first, leaving the centre to produce more. As the plant gets older, leave the outer leaves and pick only those from the centre. Both in appearance and flavour, landcress is very similar to watercress, and it makes an excellent substitute in salads.

WATERCRESS, a member of the nasturtium family, is a hardy perennial plant with smooth, round leaves, slightly hairy, crunchy stems and a strong, peppery taste. It grows naturally and profusely along streams and in springs in limestone-rich areas. Care must be exercised when picking it to ensure that it is not confused with its lookalike poisonous companion, 'marshwort' or 'foolscress', as it is sometimes called. It is important, too, that the stream or river is fresh, unpolluted and free flowing. If you are lucky enough to have a stream or river running through your garden, young rooted pieces of watercress can be planted along its banks. These rooted pieces of watercress can be taken from old plants or bought watercress whose stems have rooted. These roots can also be planted in the garden in a deep trench in wet soil, or in a clay pot or wooden fruit box filled with fertile, sandy compost and watered copiously every day.

MUSTARD, when grown as a salad crop, is generally always combined with cress and grown in exactly the same way except that it is sown several days after the cress as it germinates far more quickly.

BRASSICAS

The final group of salad leaves belongs to the family of brassicas or cabbage. Although almost any type of cabbage can be eaten when young and finely shredded, the most popular are the paler, winter cabbage varieties: the Dutch white cabbage; the hard-headed red cabbage; and the colourful, ornamental cabbages with their rounded, frilly or serrated leaves in deep purple, red and grey-green, such as 'Osaka Red and White' F1, or 'Ragged Jack'. In addition, there is an ever-increasing variety of oriental brassicas now available. Cabbages such as the solid-headed, pale green, crisp-leaf Chinese cabbage can range in shape and size from long and thin to compact and stumpy depending on the variety. They are all valued salad plants because of their winter availability, their crunchy texture and their long shelf life.

SALAD VEGETABLES

In addition to this wide variety of salad leaves, there are many other plants which bring additional life to salads through their colour, texture and flavour. Many of these are the stalks and swollen stems of edible plants such as fennel and celery. Others are edible bulbs, roots and tubers like onions, radishes, turnips, beetroot (beets), kohl-rabi,

Red cabbage

Cabbage

potatoes, carrots, parsnips and artichokes. Some are the fruits of plants like tomatoes, cucumbers, aubergines (egg-plants) and peppers. Others are vegetables which are generally served cooked, but which are also delicious and more nutritious raw, such as sweetcorn, courgettes (zucchini), leeks, turnips, mushrooms and a wide variety of peas and beans, also known as legumes. The non-leafy brassicas like Brussels sprouts, cauliflower sprouting broccoli and calabrese also make excellent salad vegetables when young with firm, tight heads.

STALKS AND STEMS

FLORENCE FENNEL, also known as bulb fennel, sweet fennel or *finocchio*, is a pretty feathery plant with fine, shimmering green foliage and an edible, swollen, leaf base which forms a bulb at ground level. It is creamy white in colour with green-tinged stalks, each tightly wrapped around each other to produce a neat, compact bulb with a crisp, firm, celery-like texture and a delicate aniseed flavour.

ABOVE Florence fennel

RIGHT A selection of salad vegetables

40

It grows to about 45 cm (18 in) high, but is best when eaten small and young. Both the bulb and foliage can be used raw or cooked in salads. Florence fennel should not be confused with the herb fennel, which is a much taller plant grown for the flavour of its foliage. It does not form a bulb and is much easier to grow than Florence fennel, which requires light, fertile, well-drained soil and plenty of sun.

CELERY is mainly grown for its long, crisp stem and distinctive fresh taste, but its leaves are also full of flavour and can be used for seasoning and garnishing. There are three main types of celery: leaf celery, self-blanching celery and blanched celery. Leaf celery grows to about 30 cm (12 in) high and has thin, delicate stems and attractive, bushy leaves. It can be eaten raw or added to cooked, savoury dishes like soups and stews. Self-blanching celery is also known as green celery as it produces very light green shoots. It is less hardy than the 'blanched' variety and is therefore grown mainly for summer and autumn use. Blanched celery, also known as 'trench' celery, is a much more robust variety, which is able to withstand severe weather conditions and therefore makes an excellent winter vegetable. It is so called because it is grown in trenches with its stem covered by earth to exclude the light, producing a white colour. Blanched celery can be used raw or cooked, but loses its bright colour and some of its texture and appearance when cooked.

CELERIAC, although introduced to Britain from Egypt in the early eighteenth century, is still little known. It is grown for its stem, which swells into a rather ugly, knobbly bulb, just above the ground. Because of its root-like appearance, it is sometimes referred to as a root vegetable. Although slightly fibrous in texture, its fine, celery-like flavour and its green, leafy head mean it is also known as 'turnip-rooted' celery. Celeriac is an excellent winter vegetable, either cooked or grated raw into salads. Celeriac rémoulade is a famous dish which uses the raw root grated or shredded finely and mixed with mayonnaise. It can also be cut into

Celery

42

very fine 'chips', deep fried and used as a tasty and decorative topping for a salad.

BULBS, ROOTS AND TUBERS

ONIONS, from the large bulb to the tiny hazelnut spheres of the Egyptian tree onion, are perhaps the most important vegetable in the kitchen both for cooked and raw dishes and, in particular, for salads. Although referred to as bulbs, they are in fact compacted layers of swollen-leaf bases in which the plant stores its food. The large bulb onions, which vary in flavour from strong to mild and in colour from white to red, add interesting taste, texture and colour to salads. The smaller shallots, pickling onions and Egyptian tree onions can all be sliced into fine rings and used for both appearance and flavour. Spring onions, also known as scallions or salad onions, are the most gentle of the onion family and have a refreshing flavour and attractive colour. Both the swollen bulb and the straight, hollow leaves are used for salads throughout the year. The strong, definite and indeed unique flavour of garlic is also invaluable to the salad maker, especially for flavouring salad oils, vinegars and dressings, for example aïoli, the garlic-flavoured mayonnaise. To impart its unique flavour directly to the salad bowl, rub a cut clove around the bowl before adding the salad ingredients.

RADISHES are very underrated, perhaps because of the generally poor quality and limited variety available in the shops. They are, however, one of the oldest cultivated vegetables in Britain and a most varied and versatile salad crop. Freshly grown and picked radishes are crisp in texture, juicy and slightly peppery in taste. They come in two shapes – round and oval – and can vary greatly in size. Small-rooted varieties are grown for use in the summer months, while large-rooted, more hardy radishes are grown in the winter. The colour, too, can vary from the pale creamy white of the Japanese summer radish to the bright red varieties like 'Sharo', 'Sparkler' and the winter radish 'China Rose'. Brown skins feature mainly in the winter varieties like 'Brown Winter' and 'Violet de Gournay'. For flavour, I choose the peppery, pink-and-white 'French Breakfast' variety. Both winter and summer varieties are quick and easy to grow and are delicious sliced into salads or just eaten as they are with salt as part of a crudités assortment. When the plants turn to seed, the seed pods, while still crisp, green and tender, can also be added to a salad.

BEETROOT, also known as 'beets', is an excellent summer vegetable and particularly versatile in salad dishes both cooked and raw. When cooked, it should be cooled slightly before being dressed with a light vinaigrette or combined with other salad vegetables. When used raw, it is generally finely shredded or grated. This root vegetable varies in shape from round to cylindrical, sometimes tapering to a point. Its colour ranges from deep purple-red to yellow and white. The red varieties are inclined to 'bleed', while the yellow and white provide a clean, sharp colour. All shapes and colours are attractive in a salad and the velvety texture is a pleasure to eat. All varieties are at their best when small and young.

CARROTS have been cultivated in Europe for thousands of years and were introduced to Britain during the reign of Quen Elizabeth I. They are now one of the most common root crops grown for both cooking and salad use. They come in all shapes and sizes depending on their variety. For an early crop of carrots which are picked when young, small, slender and smooth-skinned, 'Amsterdam' are ideal. For a slightly broader, longer carrot there is 'Nantes', and for a stumpy, conical-shaped carrot, for use as a more mature main crop, 'Chantenay Red Cored' is ideal. For a late-maturing crop, which can be used in the winter either directly from the ground or stored, 'Berlicum' and 'Autumn King' are good varieties. For flavour, the carrot is not only dependent on its variety and age, but on soil type, which should ideally be rich, fertile, light and well drained. Some people believe the best flavour to be from the quick-maturing varieties, picked small and enjoyed young, while others believe the larger, slower-maturing varieties have more depth and density. Small carrots have fresh, young leaves which can also be used raw in salads.

JERUSALEM ARTICHOKE is a very knobbly tuber which grows to about the size of a hen's egg, but in a more irregular shape. It is an excellent winter vegetable, either cooked and diced, or raw and grated and mixed with lemon juice to keep it white. It has a sweet, slightly smoky, nutty taste reminiscent of the globe artichoke, whose tender hearts can also be used raw or cooked in salads.

POTATOES are the tubers which form on the plant's underground stems. Of all the root and salad crops, it is perhaps one of the most widely eaten and used for the ever-popular dish, potato salad. Simple though it may seem, to get the best results when using potatoes in any salad dish, it is important to choose the correct type: one which will hold its shape and also have a good flavour. 'Desirée', along with 'Pink Fir Apple' are the best salad varieties.

FRUITS OR FRUITING VEGETABLES

These vegetables, as we more generally call them, are in fact fruits because it is the fruit containing the seed that we eat.

TOMATO – this fruit, a native of Peru, was introduced into Europe in the sixteenth century as the 'love apple'. It is now one of the most widely used and grown of all salad vegetables, enjoyed for its colour, taste, appearance and texture in both raw and cooked dishes. In warm, sunny climates it grows like a weed, while in more northerly areas it needs to be coaxed and cosseted a little more. Given rich, well-fertilized and drained soil, however, tall bush or dwarf tomatoes can easily be grown, with a little heat, sun and shelter. Since most varieties of tomato also lend themselves particularly well to being grown in grow-bags, boxes or pots, they are particularly useful in the small garden. There are three main types of tomato, all perfect for salads: the large Mediterranean type, sometimes known as 'beefsteak' tomatoes, which are excellent for slicing and, when grown in the sun, have a beautiful flavour, for example the 'Marmande' and 'Golden Boy' varieties; the medium-size tomato, which has a trailing, busy habit like 'Sleaford Abundance' F1; and the ordinary tall types, which can grow to over 4 m (12 ft) and which require support on a cane or stake. Varieties such as 'Ailsa Craig' and 'Alicante', two red-

Salad potatoes

skinned tomatoes, and the well-flavoured, yellow-skinned varieties like 'Golden Sunrise' and 'Yellow Perfection' are attractive additions to the salad table, as are the striped 'Tigerella' and the small, increasingly popular 'cherry' tomato like 'Gardener's Delight', with its superb flavour. They are delicious to eat and delicate and attractive in any combination of salad ingredients.

CUCUMBERS, like tomatoes, are naturally climbing or sprawling plants. They throw out long vines which can be trained to a network of strings, wires, trellis or supports. They enjoy a rich humus soil which retains moisture. This explains why they are often found scrambling over the compost heap. Although some varieties do require greenhouse conditions, most are quite happy to climb and sprawl outdoors as long as they have a sheltered, gently sunny site. There are three main types of cucumber: the 'greenhouse'

'Greenhouse' cucumber

46

cucumber, which will grow up to 30 cm (12 in) long and has smooth, rich, dark skin; the 'outdoor' or 'ridge' cucumber, which takes its name from the fact that it was originally planted on ridges; and the gherkin. The ridge cucumber is shorter in length than the greenhouse cucumber and has a slightly prickly skin; the stubby, prickly-textured gherkin is grown mainly for pickling. Cucumbers have always been an important salad vegetable, peeled or unpeeled, served as part of a mixed-leaf salad or simply dressed in yoghurt, lemon juice and chopped mint.

PEPPERS, also known as capsicums, and sweet peppers, were introduced into Europe from South America by the Spaniards. They are green when not fully mature, turning to red, yellow, orange or a deep purple-black when completely ripe. Their deliciously juicy, crispy, sharp or sweet flesh is delicious in salads, diced or cut into slivers, and their colours are so vibrant that they bring vitality to any salad arrangement. They are also excellent roasted or grilled, then marinated in fine oil and herbs. The mature peppers have a richer, sweeter taste than more immature fruit.

CHILLIES are a hot and fiery variety of pepper, with generally smaller and more tapered pods than those of the bulbous sweet pepper. Their heat ranges from mild to almost unbearably hot, with the chilli pepper becoming more fiery as it matures. This generally means that the green chilli peppers, which are less mature than the yellows and reds, are also less hot. However, colour, shape and size are

LEFT Green pepper
RIGHT Chilli peppers

not always a reliable guide to their strength. Like tomatoes, peppers – both the sweet and chilli varieties – require heat, sun, a fertile soil and a sheltered area to grow. Where the climate is right, they can grow as well outdoors as under glass; however, the results are more consistent if grown in frames or under cloches. The most successful varieties of sweet peppers are 'Bell Boy', 'Merit' and 'Prolific'. 'Long Red Cayenne' is a very prolific hot pepper.

AUBERGINES are called 'eggplants' because of the white/cream variety, which resembles an egg in shape. The most popular type, however, is the dark-skinned, deep-purple aubergine, which is at its best when its skin is smooth, unblemished and shiny. Like peppers, aubergines can be grown in cooler climates as long as they have plenty of heat and sunshine, preferably under glass or in a polythene tunnel. Two good varieties are 'Black Prince' and 'Moneymaker'. Although aubergines are unpleasant raw, they have a most interesting flavour when cooked. When sliced thinly and fried, they make an excellent addition to any salad.

OTHER VEGETABLES

COURGETTES (zucchini) are miniature, immature vegetable marrows. A member of the melon and squash family, they range in colour from dark and light mottled green to bright canary yellow, including some attractive striped varieties. Their colour and texture in salads, particularly when raw, is crisp and attractive. They are best used when small and tender, anything from 3.5 cm (1½ in) to 15.5 cm (6 in) long. Courgettes, like melons, require well-fertilized, slightly acid soil and plenty of water. The most reliable varieties are 'Zucchini' and 'Burpee Golden Zucchini', the yellow-skinned variety.

GARDEN PEAS are also known as green peas, shelling peas or petit pois. They are at their most tender and tasty when small and young and have a much better flavour raw than cooked. The young leafy shoots, flowers and tendrils of the pea are also delicious lightly steamed or raw. Two good varieties are 'Hurst Beagle' and 'Sweetness'; and for petit pois, 'Little Marvel'.

MANGETOUT (snow pea or edible podded pea) is grown for its flat pod rather than its seeds and every bit is eaten before it has a chance to grow and fill out. The best varieties are 'Carouby de Manssane' and 'Oregon Sugar Pod'. The fatter sugar snap is also eaten for its pod, the best varieties being 'Sugar Snap', 'Sugar Rae', 'Agio' and 'Sugar Bon'.

ASPARAGUS PEAS are ornamental plants grown for their winged pods which are picked when about 4 cm (1½ in) long before they become tough. The plants grow to about 38 cm (15 in) high, have delicate clover-like foliage and pretty, reddish-brown flowers. Their tendrils are particularly tasty. They can be lightly steamed and, when cold, used in salads or simply left raw.

BROAD BEANS are the oldest of all our beans, dating from as far back as the Bronze Age. They are generally always cooked, whether eaten as a hot vegetable or cold in a salad. One of the main varieties for early sowing during late autumn is 'Aquadulce Claudia', which crops during late spring. 'Imperial Green Long Pod' has an excellent flavour and is sown in the spring for the main crop, as is 'Express'.

FRENCH BEANS are one of the most popular green beans and appear in an enormous number of varieties. There is the dwarf fine bean or haricot vert intended for light steaming or eating raw, the two main kinds being the climbing variety 'Blue Lake' and the dwarf, flat-podded variety 'Limelight', as well as 'Tendergreen', the round, pencil-podded variety. Flageolets such as the 'Chevrier Vert' variety are flat-style, green French beans intended for partial drying. Haricot sec such as the 'Dutch Brown' variety are intended for complete drying and sold in packets as the familiar white or green haricot beans. They are sometimes referred to as 'navy' beans. All forms can be used in salads, the fresh green beans either cooked or raw and the dried varieties after cooking and cooling.

RUNNER BEANS are a very prolific summer vegetable. These climbing beans with their beautiful flowers and foliage are as attractive in a decorative border as on a trellis or in a vegetable plot. 'Painted Lady' with its pink and white flowers is one of the most attractive, particularly over

archways and trellis. The flavour of a runner bean is more pronounced and coarser than a French bean. They are most delicious when picked young and cooked whole or in short pieces and make excellent salads when cold.

NON LEAFY BRASSICAS

Brussels sprouts, cauliflower, sprouting broccoli and calabrese make excellent salad vegetables when young and with firm, tight heads. Brussels sprouts shred beautifully and can be used like fine cabbage to make a delicate winter slaw; cauliflower with its creamy-white head, sprouting broccoli with its clusters of flower heads, and calabrese with its spears of deep-green clusters of flower buds can all be divided into florets and incorporated in their raw state into a variety of crisp, crunchy salad dishes.

Salad herbs

Although this extensive range of salad leaves and vegetables is entirely complete on its own, a scant or liberal use of culinary herbs can enliven and enhance even the most attractive and delicious salad combination. Their aromatic leaves, the crunchy or delicate texture and the infinite variety of colour, form and flavour can transform a quite ordinary salad into something rich and exciting. Herbs such as fennel and dill can add piquancy to salads, while robustly flavoured leaves like lovage add body and an earthy quality. A touch of lemon balm or thyme brings a crisp sharpness to a mixture of delicate leaves, while chopped coriander or fenugreek evoke thoughts of the Orient. Even the distinctive smell of lightly bruised basil is reminiscent of warm, steamy days in France, Italy or Turkey.

ANGELICA is a beautiful, vigorous plant and its fresh, young leaves can be used in salads and to flavour fresh fruit *compote*. It is useful in the kitchen garden and is one of the first herbs to appear in spring. It can grow up to 3 m (10 ft) high when flowering and therefore needs to be placed so that it does not overpower the rest of the plants.

Mangetout (snow pea)

LEMON BALM, also called 'Melissa', is known for its refreshing, lemon-scented leaves which can be used whole or chopped into salads. The leaves, which are light green, golden or variegated in colour, have deep veins and jagged edges. The plant can grow up to 60 cm (24 in) tall and enjoys most types of soil and situation.

BASIL is a beautifully fragrant herb, of which there are a number of different varieties. Sweet or common basil has large, strongly flavoured, green leaves with a clove-like scent. It is excellent in salads and has a particular affinity with tomatoes. It is an essential ingredient in Italian pesto, a thick sauce of pounded basil leaves, pine nuts, olive oil, Parmesan cheese and garlic, which is traditionally served with pasta but is also wonderful with other salad leaves and ingredients. The French call it *pistou* and add it to soup. It can grow up to 60 cm (24 in) high, depending on the variety, and needs a bright, sunny position. In northern climates it really needs to be grown indoors on a warm, sunny windowsill or under glass. There are also a number of red varieties, including purple ruffle basil which has large crinkly leaves with ruffled edges, and dark opal basil which has flatter leaves with less-pronounced edges and a more spicy, gingerish flavour. Additionally, there are the dwarf or bush basils, which are also known as Greek or fine-leaved basils. They have tiny green leaves with a slightly milder flavour and are very suitable for growing in pots. Lemon-scented basil has small leaves and a delicate, lemon flavour; it is also excellent in salads.

BORAGE is a beautiful, decorative herb with dull, velvety green, hairy leaves and bright, cobalt-blue, star-shaped flowers. It grows wild in many parts of Europe and England and is known as the 'herb of courage'. Both the flowers and very young leaves have a sweet, refreshing flavour like cucumber and are used to enhance leaf salads. It grows to a height of about 45–75 cm (18–30 in) and prefers light, well-drained soil and sunlight.

CHERVIL is a sweet, aromatic herb with a mildly aniseed flavour. It is a hardy annual with lacy, fern-like foliage and

Borage

clusters of delicate white flowers. It grows to a height of 20–30 cm (8–12 in) and enjoys well-drained soil and light shade. The young leaves are delicious in salads, particularly with other young leaves. When chopped, it makes a rather grand substitute for parsley. Chervil is one of the herbs used with parsley, chives and tarragon in the mixture known as *fines herbes*. It makes an excellent herb vinegar.

CHIVES, like parsley, are one of the most widely grown and frequently used herbs both for taste and decoration. Their delicate onion flavour has been used to enhance sauces, egg and vegetable dishes and salads since the seventeenth century. The clumps should be cut often to keep new, fine leaves coming. The pretty mauve flowers also make an attractive addition to salads. Chinese or garlic chives, introduced from China and Japan, have long, flat leaves crowned with white, star-shaped flowers in summer. They can reach a height of 60 cm (24 in) when fully mature and look most decorative. Both stalks and flowers can be used in salads.

CORIANDER is a fairly hardy, easily grown annual which is best sown thickly and cut frequently, like mustard and cress. The delicate, flat, green leaves have a feathery quality, with clusters of small palish-white flowers from summer on. It can grow to a height of 30–45 cm (12–18 in). The fan-shaped leaves have an unusual and distinctive flavour and earthy pungency. The fleshy young leaves are very good added to salads. The seeds, which taste of dried orange peel, are often used to flavour lightly spiced dishes.

DILL is a hardy annual herb that has aromatic, feathery, dull green leaves with clusters of bright yellow flowers from midsummer. It prefers fertile, well-drained soil in a sheltered position with plenty of sun where it can grow to a height of 45 cm–1 m (18–36 in). Both the leaves and flowers are valuable in the salad kitchen. The leaves give a spicy taste to salads, particularly those using fish, eggs and potatoes. The flower heads are used in seasoning vinegar, pickling cucumbers, flavouring mayonnaise and marinating fish such as salmon for the Scandinavian dish gravad lax.

FENNEL, a hardy perennial plant with feathery, aromatic, green-bronze leaves and flat, full heads of sulphur-yellow flowers, makes an attractive addition to any salad creation. Small sprigs of fennel leaves and flowers are best scattered over a green salad just before serving. They can also be chopped and added to marinades, dressings and mayonnaise. The dried stalks are often used as a base on which to bake or barbecue fish or they may be burned on the barbecue to aromatize the food. The seeds are excellent added to homemade breads. Fennel prefers poor to medium, well-drained soil and a sunny site, where it will grow to a height of 1.5–2 m (5–6½ ft).

LOVAGE, like fennel, is a hardy herbaceous perennial and a tall, attractive herb which can reach a height of 60 cm–2 m (2–6 ft). Its dark green, indented glossy leaves and stalk closely resemble celery as does its flavour, which is very strong and distinctive. Torn leaves and pieces of the chopped stems can be added to a mixed-leaf salad but

LEFT Chives RIGHT Garden Cress

Lovage

should be used sparingly as their flavour can be overpowering. A good idea is to rub the salad bowl with a piece of lovage to disperse its flavour just as one would do with garlic.

MARJORAM is a tender, sweet-scented Mediterranean herb with a flavour rather like thyme. It has many forms and varieties: there is sweet or knotted marjoram, which is annual and has soft leaves; pot marjoram, which is perennial and has less fragrant leaves; and wild marjoram, which is also known as oregano. Oregano has a more pungent flavour and its leaves are a slightly darker green. It grows with abandon over the Mediterranean hillsides, flowering freely and forming thick carpets of pale pink. It requires poor soil and full sunlight and makes an excellent border plant. Both the leaves and flowers can be harvested at any time for use in mixed-leaf and tomato salads.

ABOVE Mint LEFT Gold-tipped marjoram

MINT is a hardy herbaceous perennial which has highly aromatic, oval or spear-shaped leaves and pale mauve, pink or white flowers. It is a rampant grower and can reach a height of 1 m (3 ft). To prevent it overrunning vegetable and flowerbeds, it is best planted in a container either buried in the ground, or set on a patio or veranda. There are many varieties of mint, including apple, spearmint, peppermint, gingermint, eau-de-cologne mint, and lemon mint. Mint's distinctive and cooling flavour is particularly good with cucumber, potatoes and peas and, used sparingly, makes an interesting addition to a bowl of young, mixed salad leaves.

PARSLEY is a hardy biennial plant and is one of the most important culinary herbs. Its mildly flavoured leaves, in both the common curly-type parsley and the more aromatic flat-leaf or Italian parsley, are widely used both for flavouring and decoration. The stalks have a more concentrated flavour than the heads, and are an important element in a classic bouquet garni, along with a bay leaf and a sprig of thyme. Parsley is also an important element in the mixture of finely chopped herbs referred to as *fines herbes*, along with chervil, tarragon and chives. The flat-leaf variety, torn into pieces, makes an excellent addition to a mixed-leaf salad, while both types, when chopped, bring additional flavour, colour and texture to any type of salad.

ABOVE Curly-leaf parsley

RIGHT Broad-leaf parsley

TARRAGON 'must never be excluded from salletts', according to John Evelyn, a seventeenth-century botanist. This deciduous perennial with its long, narrow, mid-green leaves and small, white, ball-shaped flowers, is highly prized for its aromatic, mildly aniseed flavour. It enjoys fertile, well-drained soil and a sheltered site in full sun. There are two forms of tarragon, the more distinctly flavoured small-leaf French variety, and the taller, coarser large-leaf Russian

tarragon. I prefer to use the French tarragon, particularly in salads, or chopped with parsley, chervil and chives for *fines herbes*, or in salad dressings and herb-flavoured vinegars.

SALAD FLOWERS

The Romans, who introduced many herbs into the kitchen, also added flowers to their culinary repertoire, understanding fully that food should be appealing not only to the taste buds, but also to the eye. Although some flowers such as nasturtiums and pot marigolds are used for their flavour, their main purpose is to provide contrast in both colour and texture. Flowers are a particularly stunning addition to salad leaves and make an excellent conversation piece.

Flowers to enhance the salad table can be both wild and cultivated. In both cases they should be clean and free from dust, dirt, and poisonous insecticides and be well-washed before use. Wild flowers like chickweed, tansy, elderflowers and broom, should only be picked if plentiful. Those protected by law, such as the English cowslip, should never be picked. Before using flowers for culinary purposes, it is important to know which are edible and which are poisonous. The following are my favourites and they are all edible. For further information on wild flowers, a specialist book should be consulted. Small flowers, and those with no hard parts, can be used whole, but others like daisies and chrysanthemums should have their petals removed and sprinkled over the salad after it has been dressed and just before serving.

BORAGE flowers are star-shaped and brilliant cobalt blue in colour. They look delightful strewn on vegetable and fruit salads, and taste slightly sweet. The hairy sepals behind the petals should be removed.

BERGAMOT flowers, with their scarlet, tubular blooms, have an aromatic, minty-lemon taste and look stunning in a mixed-leaf salad.

CHIVE flowers, with their attractive mauve colour, make colourful additions to salads, either in whole heads or individual petals.

CHRYSANTHEMUM leaves and petals have a slightly pungent flavour and can be scattered through a leafy salad. The petals should only be removed from the flower head after it has been dipped in boiling water.

DAISIES, both the white lawn and field varieties, can be used whole in salads to create an attractive assembly. They should be picked in the sunshine when their petals are open and they look most attractive. The petals of the larger, cultivated varieties can be pulled off and sprinkled over salads, adding a splash of colour to any salad dish.

ABOVE Chamomile OPPOSITE Nasturtiums

ELDERFLOWER, with its delightful, lacy, sweet-smelling blossoms composed of tiny confetti-like flowers and distinctive muscatel flavour, makes an attractive addition to a salad bowl in early summer.

GERANIUM leaves, green or variegated, and the white or pale pink flowers of the geranium plant can be added to salads, not only to impart flavour but also to add interest in colour and texture. The most pungent varieties are rose, peppermint, pineapple, orange and lemon.

LAVENDER'S tiny purplish-blue flowers can be used in salads; however, their flavour is strong and they should, therefore, be used sparingly.

LOBELIA'S pretty white, pink and blue flowers with their bell-shaped blossoms have a slightly sweet smell reminiscent of honeysuckle. They look particularly attractive tossed through a salad.

POT MARIGOLD (calendula) is a hardy annual with tongue-shaped leaves and daisy-like flowers in all shades of orange, yellow and cream. It makes a tasty and colourful addition to a green salad. The young, peppery leaves add spice to a salad of mild young leaves. Only pot marigolds should be used and not confused with African or French marigolds.

NASTURTIUM is a hardy annual plant available in trailing and dwarf form and has peppery-flavoured, round, green, plain or variegated leaves and pretty trumpet-shaped orange, yellow and red flowers. It makes an attractive salad plant. The leaves add a sharp taste to a salad and the flowers a peppery piquancy, as well as a sparkling brilliance. The spurs must be picked off the flowers before they are used. Both the flowers and leaves have been used in salads for a long time. In the eighteenth century Hannah Glass wrote in her recipe for 'Salmagundy': 'throw nasturtium flowers about the cress.'

PANSY, a pretty perennial which can flower almost all year round, brings constant interest to salads. Its velvety texture and marvellous range of colours can transform a salad. The small varieties can be used whole.

PRIMROSE, with its bright yellow flowers, can be used whole in salads. The green calyx of the primrose flower is pulled away from the yellow corolla before using.

Many other flowers are edible and can also be used in salads. Here are the names of a few of the most common: chamomile, clover, cornflower, cowslip, courgette (zucchini), dandelion, honeysuckle, rose, sage, violet, lovage, rosemary, thyme, day lily, and chicory flowers.

CHAPTER THREE

SALAD RECIPES

*T*he Romans had a wonderful saying concerning salad making: 'It takes four people to make a salad – a miser to put in the vinegar, a spendthrift to add the oil, a wise man to season it and a madman to toss it.' The following recipes contain all these ingredients in varying degrees, influenced by many different countries and individual personalities, from Roman times to the present day. They are a collection combining all that is good and fine from the salad and vegetable garden – mixed-leaf and green salads, leaf and vegetable salads, and leaves combined with all sorts of other ingredients, from meat and fish to bread and cheese. They are colourful concoctions to tempt the palate and to entice the eye: salads to start and end a meal with, salads for a snack or main dish, salads for summer and winter, indeed, salads for every occasion.

ALL THE RECIPES SERVE 4 AS A MAIN COURSE UNLESS OTHERWISE STATED.

FOLLOW EITHER METRIC, IMPERIAL OR US MEASURES FOR THE RECIPES, NOT A MIXTURE.

ALL SPOON MEASURES GIVEN ARE FOR EITHER METRIC OR IMPERIAL MEASURING SPOONS,
WHICH GIVE ACCURATE MEASUREMENTS.

A simple mixed leaf salad decorated
with marigold leaves.

*C*LASSIC

GREEN SALAD

A green salad can be as simple or as complex as you like, depending on taste, season and availability. Salad leaves of all types can be used to fill a salad bowl, with colours that range from bright chartreuse to golden bronze, with every shade of green, pink and purple in between and a variety of shapes and textures. When a collection of mixed leaves is being used as the main part of the salad rather than as an accompaniment or a garnish 40–50 g (1½–2 oz, a large handful) of leaves is required for each person. Where the green salad is used as an accompaniment, allow approximately 25 g (1 oz, a medium handful) per person.

Wash the salad leaves carefully under cold running water, dry in a salad basket or spinner before combining in a large salad bowl. Serve the salad tossed in a light dressing, such as champagne dressing (p. 113), a classic vinaigrette or its variations (pp. 108–9), or a more elaborate dressing (pp. 112–13).

Mesclun Salad

Mesclun is the Provençal name for a mixture of small delicate salad leaves such as rocket (arugula), lamb's lettuce, oak-leaf lettuce, curly endive (frisée), romaine, red radicchio, dandelion, small leaves of cos lettuce and sprigs of herbs such as chervil and flat-leaf parsley. These leaves are very easy to grow either as individual crops or as a mixed crop, where several varieties are grown together. They are cropped by cutting a few leaves at a time as required, allowing the plants to continue to grow and produce further crops. Such salad mixtures are often described as 'saladisi' or a cut-and-come-again crop. Serve the salad tossed in a light dressing, such as a classic vinaigrette or hazelnut dressing (p. 109).

A NOVEMBER SALLET

In the winter when the wide variety of delicate salad leaves is no longer available, a mixed-leaf salad relies on more hardy leaves, such as lamb's lettuce, landcress, winter purslane, red 'Salad Bowl', sorrel, spinach and chard, watercress, cabbage, and oriental greens, such as Chinese cabbage and pak choi, along with members of the chicory family, including both the curly-leaf endive (frisée) and the broad-leaf Batavian (escarole). The combination can be large or small depending on availability, with fresh herbs and edible winter flowers, like viola and marigold, added for interest as well as a splash of colour. For these more substantial leaves I use a more robust dressing, such as herb dressing (p. 109), walnut dressing (p. 112), or chilli and black bean dressing (p. 113).

SERVES 4

75 g (3 oz, 1 large bunch) young spinach or sorrel leaves

1 small head of chicory (Belgian endive)

100 g (4 oz, 1 small head) Chinese leaves

50–75 g (2–3 oz, 1 medium bunch) winter purslane

2–4 tablespoons dressing (see above)

Prepare the salad leaves. Remove the central stalk from the spinach or sorrel if necessary and carefully wash and dry. Tear into pieces if too large. Trim the hard end of the chicory, slice the head through its length and separate the leaves, removing the bitter core. Remove any damaged leaves from the Chinese cabbage and tear or shred the rest into pieces. Wash and dry the purslane.

Combine all the salad leaves in a large bowl. Sprinkle over the dressing and toss lightly. If flowers or herbs are being added, scatter over the salad and serve immediately.

A WILD COUNTRY SALAD

In early summer, when the countryside is bursting with new life and many young tender leaves and herbs are appearing in the hedgerows as well as in gardens, the salad bowl not only takes on a whole new appearance, but provides many hours of enjoyment, in the quest for the most succulent and interesting leaves. Those to look out for in backyards, parks, meadows and country lanes are: wild sorrel, dandelion, purslane, miner's lettuce, landcress and watercress, to name but a few. If a totally wild salad is, however, not practical, then a selection of young cultivated salad leaves makes an excellent alternative. These mixed country leaves are best served simply with a light olive or nut oil, like hazelnut or almond, and either a wedge of lemon or a little elderflower or herb vinegar on the side.

SERVES 1

A selection of young salad leaves, approx. 40–50 g (1½–2 oz, 1 large handful), either wild or cultivated or a mixture of both chosen from the following:

spring saladings (lamb's lettuce, oak-leaf lettuce, curly endive [frisée] – the yellow centre – rocket [arugula] and young spinach leaves); wild leaves (sorrel, dandelion, landcress, watercress, nasturtium leaves and purslane); herbs (mint, fennel, chervil, basil, tarragon, oregano and marjoram); flowers (borage, pansies, marigolds and thyme flowers).

1 spring onion (scallion), white and green part, finely chopped

15 g (½ oz, 1 tablespoon) sunflower seeds, toasted

DRESSING

Extra virgin olive oil or hazelnut oil

Elderflower or herb vinegar

Carefully select and wash the salad leaves and dry well in a salad spinner or basket. Wash and dry the herbs and flowers, taking care not to damage them. Arrange the leaves, herbs and flowers together in a loose pile on a large plate, making sure that each is shown to its best advantage and that there is a good balance of colour and texture. Sprinkle over the chopped onion and sunflower seeds. Serve the oil and vinegar separately.

WATERCRESS, CHICORY AND NASTURTIUM
SALAD WITH ROASTED PECAN NUTS

The generic word for nasturtium is also the botanical name for watercress and, as both are spicy, peppery greens, they combine well in the salad bowl. The chicory (Belgian endive) is crisp, juicy and slightly bitter and makes a refreshing contrast to the peppery leaves. The brightly coloured blossoms of the nasturtium flowers spike the arrangement with lively bursts of colour. Walnuts can be used as an alternative to pecan nuts.

SERVES 4

1 teaspoon walnut oil

25–50 g (1–2 oz, $\frac{1}{4}$ cup) pecan nuts

2 bunches watercress, approx. 350 g (12 oz, $\frac{3}{4}$ lb)

3 firm heads chicory (Belgian endive)

16 small nasturtium leaves

6 nasturtium flowers, petals separated

8 whole nasturtium flowers to garnish

6 tablespoons walnut and shallot dressing (p. 112)

Heat the walnut oil in a frying pan, add the pecan nuts and toss over a medium heat until lightly toasted. Leave to cool.

Wash the watercress well under cold running water. Discard the thick hairy stems and break the watercress branches into smaller pieces. Dry well in a salad spinner or basket. Trim off the hard base of the chicory (Belgian endive), divide each piece lengthwise into quarters, and cut out the core. Separate the leaves. Wash the nasturtium leaves and flowers, removing their stems. Leave the leaves whole, but shred six of the flowers.

Combine the prepared leaves, shredded flowers and nuts in a large bowl. Pour the dressing over the salad and toss lightly. Divide between four plates, piling the leaves high in the centre, but letting them fall loosely towards the edge. Arrange the whole nasturtium flowers casually on the salad. Serve immediately.

VARIATIONS

Segments of ruby-red grapefruit or blood oranges arranged through the leaves and served with crusty bread sticks makes a delightful salad for a first course. Alternatively, serve with slices of pear and blue cheese, such as Roquefort, Stilton or Gorgonzola, and accompanied by crusty country bread for an excellent main course.

Mixed leaf and vegetable salad

Although there are many recipes for salads combining leaves and vegetables, I find the most rewarding are those inspired by the produce of the seasons. Because of the many permutations of ingredients, they are best simply dressed.

SERVES 4

2 medium-size, firm, waxy potatoes

65 ml (2½ fl oz, 5 tablespoons) white wine

1 large red and green pepper

1 small red salad onion, sliced into rings

3 artichoke hearts, cooked and sliced into rings

16 black olives, stoned

175 g (6 oz, ¼–½ lb to taste) fine green beans

1 small cos lettuce

1 small lollo rosso

1 handful of mixed leaves (purslane, rocket, basil and landcress)

2 firm tomatoes, quartered

8 tablespoons vinaigrette or citrus dressing (pp. 108–9)

eggs, hard boiled and quartered

8 nasturtium flowers and small leaves

16 borage flowers

Boil the potatoes in their skins until just tender, drain, slice into 5 mm (¼ in) rings, transfer to a large bowl and pour over the white wine. Cut the peppers in half, brush lightly with oil and grill until the skin blisters and burns. Peel, remove the seeds and cut the flesh into long, thin strips. Add to the potatoes with the salad onions, artichoke hearts and black olives. Cook the beans until just tender, then refresh until cold under running water. Drain and dry before adding to the other ingredients. Divide the lettuce into leaves and wash and dry along with the remaining leaves. Add the salad leaves and tomatoes to the salad bowl. Drizzle the dressing over the salad and toss gently to coat all the ingredients. Arrange the egg through the leaves. Decorate with the flowers. Serve immediately.

VARIATIONS

Thin fingers of cooked beef or chicken, along with any assortment of cooked vegetables in fine strips, can be added to the basic leaves to create a substantial main course salad.

73

Dandelion and Sorrel Salad

WITH NEW POTATOES, BACON AND CROÛTONS

Dandelions and wood sorrel are two plants that not only grow wild, but can also be cultivated for use in the kitchen. Dandelion plants grown specifically for salads are blanched under a flowerpot to make them less bitter. They have a similar taste to curly endive (frisée), which makes an excellent substitute if young tender dandelion leaves are not available. Young sorrel has a sharp, astringent flavour, which combines well with the dandelion's bitterness.

SERVES 4

275 g (10 oz , 3½ large bunches) young dandelion leaves
or curly endive (frisée)

50 g (2 oz, a large handful) wood sorrel or sorrel leaves

12–16 tiny new potatoes, scrubbed

7.5 cm (3 in) piece of narrow baguette loaf (French stick)

6 tablespoons extra virgin olive oil

175 g (6 oz, 8 thick slices) back bacon, cut into 2.5 cm (1 in) strips

1–2 cloves garlic, crushed

½ teaspoon Dijon mustard

1 tablespoon white wine vinegar

Salt and freshly ground black pepper

Wash the dandelion, or curly endive (frisée), leaves and the sorrel in plenty of cold water, then dry in a salad spinner or basket.

Cook the potatoes in boiling water over a medium heat for about 8 minutes, or until just tender. Drain and keep warm.

Cut the bread into very thin slices and fry in 3 tablespoons of the oil until crisp and golden in colour. Remove from the pan and drain. Fry the strips of bacon until crisp, then remove from the pan and keep warm.

Put the crushed garlic in the bottom of a salad bowl and blend with the mustard and wine vinegar. Season with salt and freshly ground black pepper and gradually blend in the remaining oil to make the dressing. Add the warm potatoes to the bowl and coat in the dressing, then add the dandelion and sorrel leaves. Toss gently to coat well. Scatter the bacon over the salad along with the croûtons of bread and serve immediately.

VARIATIONS

Curly endive (frisée) can be used instead of dandelion leaves, and spinach instead of sorrel. The potatoes can be omitted for a less substantial salad.

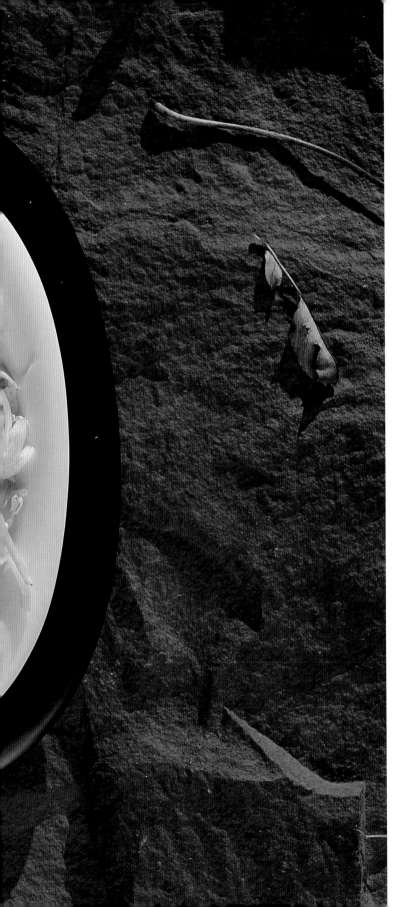

*O*RIENTAL SALAD WITH

MIXED LEAVES

This refreshing yet substantial salad based on Chinese cabbage – also known as Chinese leaves or Shantung cabbage – sprouted beans, fine green beans and broad beans, tossed in a spicy oriental dressing makes an ideal main course for serious salad eaters.

SERVES 4

1 small head Chinese leaves, approx. 225–275 g (8–10 oz, ½ lb)

175 g (6 oz, 2½ cups) fresh bean sprouts (p. 27) or sprouted beans

6 spring onions (scallions), white and green part

1 small head fennel, thinly sliced

175 g (6 oz, ¼–½ lb to taste) fine green beans

100 g (4 oz, ¼ lb) broad beans

3–4 tablespoons oriental dressing (p. 112)

8 sprigs of chervil or coriander

Shred the head of Chinese leaves coarsely and wash well under cold running water. Dry in a salad spinner or basket. Wash the bean sprouts and shake dry without breaking. Trim the spring onions (scallions) and cut into 4–5 cm (1½–2 in) lengths. Combine the leaves, bean sprouts, spring onions (scallions) and thinly sliced fennel in a large salad bowl.

Top and tail the green beans and cook in boiling water with the broad beans for about 3–4 minutes until just tender. Drain and, while still warm, toss with 2 tablespoons of the oriental dressing. Leave to go cold.

Toss the salad leaves, bean sprouts, fennel and spring onions with the remaining dressing. Divide these between four large plates, arranging them loosely over the whole area, but leaving a clear 5 cm (2 in) band around the edge of the plate. Pile the beans in a pyramid in the centre of the leaves, garnish with a few leaves of chervil and serve immediately.

*C*UCUMBER MOUSSE

This light, delicately flavoured mousse makes an ideal summer salad, served either on its own with a selection of mixed leaves and a garnish of fine sticks of cucumber, or as an accompaniment to cold poached salmon, prawns (shrimp) or crab. This recipe was given to me by my friend Ann Macfarlane.

SERVES 8–12

1 cucumber, approx. 375 g (13 oz, ¾ lb)

225 g (8 oz, ½ lb) natural cottage cheese

150 ml (5 fl oz, ⅔ cup) mayonnaise (p. 114)

½ teaspoon salt

Freshly ground black pepper

1 teaspoon caster sugar

10 g (½ oz, 2 teaspoons) powdered gelatine or

1 × 11 g (0.4 oz) sachet

150 ml (5 fl oz, ⅔ cup) cold water

150 ml (5 fl oz, ⅔ cup) double cream, lightly whipped

Watercress leaves to garnish

Peel the cucumber, cut in half lengthwise and scoop out the seeds with the point of a teaspoon. Finely chop the cucumber flesh. Press the cottage cheese through a sieve into a large mixing bowl. Add the mayonnaise, salt, freshly ground pepper and sugar.

Soak the gelatine in a teacup in four tablespoons of the measured water. Set the cup in a small saucepan holding about 2.5 cm (1 in) hot water and dissolve over a low heat until clear. Slowly pour into the cheese and mayonnaise mixture, stirring all the time. Stir in the remaining water along with the chopped cucumber. When the mixture begins to thicken and shows signs of setting, fold in the cream.

Pour into a 900 ml (1½ pint, 4-cup) ring mould or small, lightly-oiled individual moulds, each holding approx. 85 ml (3 fl oz, ⅓ cup), and chill until set.

Turn out and garnish with fine julienne sticks of cucumber tossed in a herb vinaigrette (p. 109) or watercress.

CRUDITÉS

This collection of crunchy raw vegetables is one of the most simple and attractive of all vegetable salads, made elaborate only by the various dips, dressings and sauces with which it can be served. Vinaigrette, garlic or herb mayonnaise and aïoli are just a few of the many that can be used (see pp. 108–115). A selection of two or three is ideal.

Firm, well-washed and dried vegetables and leaves, such as carrots, cucumber, peppers, fennel, chicory (Belgian endive), spring onions (scallions) and lettuce hearts, can be cut into finger-length pieces, sticks or chunks; tight-headed vegetables, such as broccoli or cauliflower, can be broken into florets; small vegetables, like mushrooms, cherry tomatoes, baby sweetcorn, courgettes (zucchini), mange-touts (snow peas), fine green beans and radishes, can be left whole.

Crudités can be served as a first course, a light lunch or a snack with crusty bread. The quantity and variety of the vegetables and dressings are a matter of personal choice and individual requirements. However, I generally allow a total of 100–150 g (4–5 oz, ¼ lb) of about five to eight different varieties of vegetables per person for a first course. The prepared vegetables are arranged in a decorative or informal way on either a large serving plate or individual plates, and the dressing, sauce or dip is served separately.

WARM SPRING VEGETABLE SALAD
IN HERB VINAIGRETTE

This salad is the perfect way to celebrate the harvest of the first spring vegetables when they are bursting with colour and flavour. Choose an assortment of whatever small, young, tender vegetables are available to make an attractive presentation that is varied in colour, taste, shape and texture: asparagus tips, cut into 5 cm (2 in) lengths; peeled baby carrots; small red radishes; baby turnips; small spring onions (scallions); small artichoke bottoms; small mange-touts (snow peas); fine green beans; baby sweetcorn; broccoli; florets of cauliflower; freshly shelled peas and beans; and skinned cherry tomatoes. I try to use a selection of at least six differently shaped and coloured vegetables, allowing a total of 225–275 g (8–10 oz, ½ lb) per person.

Wash and trim the vegetables, then cook each separately, either by steaming or boiling, until just tender. This is necessary as each vegetable will undoubtedly require a different cooking time. After cooking, drain the vegetables and refresh under cold running water to 'set' their colour. Drain well again to retain their flavour and prevent them from being watery.

Reheat the cooked vegetables, either by steaming or tossing in a little melted, unsalted butter over a low heat without colouring. Drain once again, then toss in a few tablespoons of a light herb vinaigrette (p. 109). Arrange attractively on large individual plates and garnish with finely chopped coriander, tarragon and sprigs of chervil.

Celeriac Rémoulade with Avocado and Mixed Leaf Salad

Raw celeriac cut into julienne strips makes an excellent winter salad, either as a first or main course. The rémoulade sauce used to dress the celeriac is not a true rémoulade (which contains chopped pickled dill cucumbers and capers), but rather a rich mayonnaise heavily flavoured with Dijon mustard. The following recipe is for four main course servings. Reduce the quantities by half for a first course. The rémoulade sauce is also excellent with crudités (p. 81).

SERVES 4

2 large heads celeriac

1 lemon, cut in half

175–225 g (6–8 oz, ½ lb) mixed salad leaves

2 avocados, firm but ripe

RÉMOULADE SAUCE

300 ml (10 fl oz, 1¼ cups) thick mayonnaise (p. 114)

1–2 tablespoons Dijon mustard

Squeeze of lemon juice

Freshly ground black pepper

Peel the celeriac thickly, removing the tough outer skin. There should be about 350 g (12 oz, ¾ lb) useable celeriac left after peeling. Cut in thin slices, about 3 mm (⅛ in) thick, and rub the cut surfaces with the cut lemon to prevent discolouring, Cut into thin sticks, about 5 cm (2 in) long and 3 mm (⅛ in) thick. The celeriac can also be prepared using the julienne blade or coarse-shredding blade of a food processor.

Combine the ingredients for the rémoulade sauce in a large bowl, stir to blend well, then add the prepared celeriac.

Divide the washed and dried salad leaves between four large plates and pile the celeriac rémoulade in the centre.

Peel the avocados and, using a broad-bladed swivel vegetable peeler, remove strips as if peeling an apple. Sprinkle with lemon juice. Arrange the avocado on the lettuce leaves and serve immediately.

VARIATIONS

For a less elaborate version, the celeriac rémoulade can be piled on a piece of crispy toasted bread and served simply with a salad of mixed leaves moistened with the smallest amount of vinaigrette.

CAESAR SALAD

This classic American salad, created by Caesar Cardini in the 1920s, has as many variations as there are types of lettuce. Traditionally, however, the main ingredients are hearts of cos lettuce, fine olive oil, lemon juice, Worcestershire sauce, salt and pepper, fresh Parmesan cheese, garlic-flavoured croûtons and a very lightly boiled egg. The success of the salad is in the quality of the ingredients and the mixing, which should be gentle enough to coat the leaves without bruising them.

SERVES 4

2 large heads cos lettuce

75 g (3 oz, ½ cup) GARLIC CROÛTONS

3 slices white bread, approx. 5 mm (¼ in) thick

2 cloves garlic, peeled and crushed

4–5 tablespoons olive oil

CAESAR DRESSING

2 eggs

6 tablespoons olive oil

Salt and freshly ground black pepper

Juice of 1 small lemon

1 teaspoon Worcestershire sauce

25 g (1 oz, ⅓ cup) Parmesan cheese, freshly grated

Strip the lettuce leaves carefully from the stalk, discarding any damaged outer leaves. Use whole leaves, no more than 15 cm (6 in) in length. Each main course serving will require about ten leaves. Save the remaining leaves for another salad. Wash and dry the leaves and place in a plastic bag in the refrigerator until required.

Prepare the garlic croûtons: remove the crusts from the bread and cut into 5 mm (¼ in) cubes. Put the crushed garlic in a heavy bowl and pound to a smooth paste with the end of a rolling pin or use a pestle and mortar. Gradually dribble in the oil. Leave to infuse for as long as possible. The flavour of the oil will obviously deepen the longer it sits before using. Strain the oil into a frying pan and heat. Add the bread cubes and stir to coat them evenly with the oil. Transfer the croûtons to a shallow baking sheet and bake in a hot oven at 220°C (425°F, gas mark 7) for 4–5 minutes, shaking the tray occasionally to redistribute and ensure even browning. Drain and leave aside until required.

Prepare the dressing: put the eggs in a saucepan of boiling water, return to the boil and boil for 1 minute exactly. Remove from the water immediately and break into a large wide wooden salad bowl, scraping out the thin layer of cooked white near the shell. Gradually add the oil, whisking constantly. Season with salt and pepper and whisk in the lemon juice and Worcestershire sauce. Add the lettuce to the bowl, along with almost all of the Parmesan cheese and the croûtons and toss lightly. Arrange the salad on large plates, sprinkle with the remaining Parmesan cheese and serve immediately. For illustration, see following page.

TOMATO, MOZZARELLA AND PESTO SALAD

One of the most wonderful summer combinations is Mediterranean plum tomatoes, or other sweet fragrant tomatoes, genuine Italian buffalo mozzarella cheese (not always easy to come by) and a rich pesto sauce made from fresh basil leaves, olive oil and pine nuts. Pesto sauce is available fresh or in jars, but commercially prepared pesto lacks the bright colour and fresh taste of the homemade variety. It also needs to be thinned down with olive oil before using. The whole arrangement, served with fresh crusty bread, makes an ideal first or light main course.

SERVES 4

4–8 large well-flavoured tomatoes

250–350 g (9–12 oz, ¾ lb) mozzarella cheese

225 g (8 oz, ½ lb) small, mildly-flavoured green leaves

(such as green oak-leaf, landcress, lamb's lettuce or butterhead

[Boston] lettuce)

Basil leaves to garnish

250 ml (8 fl oz, 1 cup) PESTO SAUCE

6 tablespoons chopped fresh basil leaves,

about 20 g (¾ oz)

1 large clove garlic, peeled and crushed

50 g (2 oz, ½ cup) pine nuts

Juice of 1 lemon

150 ml (5 fl oz, ⅔ cup) olive oil

Wash and dry the tomatoes and cut into slices. Slice the mozzarella thinly. Wash and dry the salad leaves in a salad spinner or basket. Prepare the pesto sauce by combining the washed and spun basil leaves, garlic, pine nuts and lemon juice in the bowl of a liquidizer or food processor. Blend until a smooth paste is formed, then gradually add the oil to make a thick sauce. Add extra oil if necessary to produce the required consistency. Arrange alternate slices of tomato and mozzarella on a large salad plate and garnish with the mixed salad leaves and pesto sauce.

CROSTINI WITH TAPENADE, GOAT'S CHEESE AND SALAD OF MIXED LEAVES

Crostini are slices of bread, 2–2.5 cm ($\frac{3}{4}$–1 in) thick, with or without the crusts, baked in the oven until crisp and used as a base for an innumerable variety of toppings, in this case tapenade and goat's cheese. Tapenade, a rich purée of capers, olives and anchovies, is spread on the crostini, covered with a slice of goat's or other distinctive cheese and baked in the oven. It is then served with mixed salad leaves as either a first or main course or a snack.

SERVES 4

8 thick slices of bread, approx. 7.5–9 cm (3–3$\frac{1}{2}$ in) thick

Olive oil

250 ml (8 fl oz, 1 cup) tapenade (p. 114)

8 × 5 mm ($\frac{1}{4}$ in) slices goat's cheese, approx. 225–350 g (8–12 oz, $\frac{1}{2}$–$\frac{3}{4}$ lb)

225 g (8 oz, $\frac{1}{2}$ lb) mixed salad leaves in season (such as curly endive [frisée], lollo rosso, red and green oak-leaf and lamb's lettuce)

2 tablespoons vinaigrette (p. 108)

1 roasted red and yellow pepper, skinned, deseeded and cut into fine julienne strips

Generously brush both sides of the bread with olive oil and set on a lightly oiled baking tray. Bake in a preheated oven at 200°C (400°F, gas mark 6) for about 8–10 minutes until crisp and golden, turning once. Spread the tapenade paste generously on each piece of toasted bread, place two slices of cheese on top and return to the oven until the cheese is melted and bubbling and the bread and tapenade are very hot. This will take about 10 minutes.

Wash and dry the salad leaves and arrange on one side of four large plates. Set two pieces of crostini slightly overlapping and just resting on the edge of the leaves. Drizzle a little vinaigrette over the leaves and scatter the fine strips of roasted pepper on top. Serve immediately.

WILD MUSHROOM SALAD WITH LEAFY GREENS AND POACHED EGG

With a renewed interest in gathering food from the countryside, this wild mushroom salad not only becomes a delicious dish to eat, but an exciting one to prepare as whatever wild local mushrooms are available can be used in its creation. Cooked in butter and flavoured with white wine and saffron, they surround a salad of lightly dressed greens topped with a poached egg. For illustration, see following page.

SERVES 4

225 g (8 oz, $\frac{1}{2}$ lb) mixed salad leaves (such as curly endive [frisée], little gem hearts, oak-leaf, lollo rosso and radicchio), according to seasonal availability

225–350 g (8–12 oz, $\frac{1}{2}$–$\frac{3}{4}$ lb) wild mushrooms, washed and dried

25 g (1 oz, 2 tablespoons) unsalted butter

2 tablespoons olive oil

8 tablespoons dry white wine

Pinch saffron threads

4 lightly poached eggs

4 tablespoons vinaigrette dressing (p. 108)

Chervil leaves to garnish

Wash the salad leaves under cold running water and dry in a salad spinner or basket. Slice the mushrooms roughly and fry in the hot butter and oil over a gentle heat until their juices are just beginning to flow. Add the wine and the saffron, shaking well to combine the flavours.

Poach the eggs until lightly cooked. Meanwhile put the salad leaves into a bowl and toss lightly with the vinaigrette. Divide the leaves between four large plates, arranging them in the centre like a posy. Using a slotted spoon, remove the hot mushrooms from the pan, set these around the edge of the leaves and coat with the cooking liquid. Remove the eggs and set one on top of the leaves on each plate. Garnish with fresh chervil and serve immediately.

Warm Salad of Monk Fish

WITH ROASTED PINE KERNELS

The firm meaty flesh of fried monkfish and soft young leaves make fine salad companions. The salad leaves should reflect the season and availability and be chosen for their colour and.appearance as much as for their flavour.

SERVES 4

750 g (1½ lb) monkfish tail, skinned and filleted

25 g (1 oz, 3 tablespoons) pine kernels

225 g (8 oz, ½ lb) mixed salad leaves (such as curly endive [frisée], lollo rosso, oak-leaf, watercress, lamb's lettuce and radicchio)

2 tablespoons oil

15 g (½ oz, 1½ tablespoons) unsalted butter

Salt and freshly ground black pepper

4 tablespoons nut oil vinaigrette (p. 109) for a light dressing, or teriyaki dressing (p. 113) for a more spicy flavour

4 sprigs fresh chervil

Cut the monkfish fillets into 24 pieces. Spread the pine kernels on a baking tray and toast under a hot grill until an even golden colour. Wash and dry the salad leaves and toss together with the pine kernels in a salad bowl.

Heat the oil and butter in a large frying pan, season the fish with salt and pepper and fry for about 1–1½ minutes on each side, turning only once. If using salmon, cook for 30 seconds on each side. For scallops, cook for 30 seconds, tossing them occasionally. Remove the fish from the pan and keep warm while finishing the salad.

Pour the vinaigrette over the leaves and toss well. Divide between four large plates. Arrange the pieces of warm fish amongst the leaves, garnish with the chervil and serve immediately.

VARIATIONS

Other flavoursome fish, such as salmon, scallops and mussels, are elegant alternatives to monkfish.

RUSSIAN SALAD WITH POACHED
CHICKEN BREAST ON MIXED LEAVES

A true Russian salad combines the best in tender young vegetables carefully chosen to make the best combination of taste, colour and texture, the total quantity of mixed vegetables never being more than half the quantity of beetroot (beets), the main vegetable. The vegetables are cut in 5 mm ($\frac{1}{4}$ in) dice and are all lightly cooked. While still warm they are tossed in vinaigrette before being coated in mayonnaise. The salad is then served in the centre of a bed of mixed leaves and decorated with thin slices of poached chicken breast.

SERVES 4

225 g (8 oz, $\frac{1}{2}$ lb) beetroot (beets), peeled

50 g (2 oz, 1 small) carrot

50 g (2 oz, 1 small) potato

1 celery stick, 50 g (2 oz)

3 tablespoons peas

4–5 tablespoons vinaigrette (p. 108)

Freshly ground black pepper

1 tablespoon chives, finely chopped

5 tablespoons thick mayonnaise (p. 114)

175 g (6 oz, 2 large bunches) mixed salad leaves as available

4 small cooked chicken breasts, approx. 75–100 g (3–4 oz, $\frac{1}{4}$ lb), cut into thin slices

Peel the beetroot (beets), cut into dice and cook in boiling water for 10 minutes until just tender, drain and put in a large mixing bowl. Peel and dice the carrot and also cook in boiling water for approximately 10 minutes, then drain. Peel the potato, dice and cook for 15–20 minutes, then drain. Dice the celery stick and cook for 10 minutes, then drain. Cook the peas for 3–5 minutes, then drain. Combine all the vegetables in a large bowl and toss in two tablespoons of the vinaigrette. Leave to go cold. Season with the pepper and chives and coat in the mayonnaise.

Wash and dry the salad leaves and divide between four large individual plates. Pile the Russian salad in the centre of the leaves and either lay the slices of chicken breast on top, or arrange amongst the leaves. Drizzle the remaining vinaigrette over the salad leaves and serve immediately.

SMOKED COUNTRY HAM WITH SALAD
OF SPRING VEGETABLES
IN HEATHER HONEY DRESSING

The combination of delicately smoked Parma or West-phalian ham and tiny, lightly cooked spring vegetables and fresh, young salad leaves moistened with a heather honey vinaigrette, makes a delightfully refreshing and elegant main course salad. Choose the tiniest, most tender and flavoursome vegetables available, such as carrots, turnips, mangetouts (snow peas), broad beans, asparagus, sweetcorn, fine green beans, radishes and spring onions (scallions).

SERVES 4

450 g (1 lb) mixed baby vegetables as available, or finely
prepared larger vegetables

225 g (8 oz, $\frac{1}{2}$ lb) young salad leaves (curly endive [frisée], lamb's
lettuce, radicchio and lollo rosso etc., as available)

8 thin slices Parma ham

HEATHER HONEY DRESSING

150 ml (5 fl oz, $\frac{2}{3}$ cup) dry white wine

3 tablespoons champagne vinegar

1 teaspoon balsamic vinegar

2 tablespoons finely chopped shallot

Pinch saffron powder (optional)

1 teaspoon heather honey

50 ml (2 fl oz, $\frac{1}{4}$ cup) extra virgin olive oil

50 ml (2 fl oz, $\frac{1}{4}$ cup) sunflower oil

Salt and freshly ground black pepper

Wash, peel and trim the vegetables. Cook each one separately until tender, either by boiling or steaming. When just tender, refresh under cold running water until stone cold. Drain and dry and put in a large mixing bowl. Wash and dry the salad leaves and keep in a plastic bag in the refrigerator until required.

Make the dressing: combine the wine, vinegars and shallot in a saucepan, bring to the boil and continue to cook quickly until the liquid has reduced by half. Remove from the heat and add the honey. Stir until dissolved. Add the saffron. Whisk in the oils until blended and season with salt and pepper.

Divide the salad leaves between four plates, arranging them in a heap in the centre of each plate. Loosely wrap two slices of ham around each pile of leaves to enclose it. Toss the vegetables in the dressing and arrange them amongst the leaves and around the edge of each plate. Drizzle a little dressing over the leaves and spoon a little over the vegetables around the edge of the dish. Serve immediately.

BEEF AND GARLIC GALETTE
WITH GREEN LENTIL DRESSING

This strongly flavoured beef and mayonnaise mould created by my chef, Paul Clarke, not only makes a perfect salad dish but is an excellent way to use up an excess of cooked roast beef. The lentil salad, which can be made from yellow or green lentils, moistened with oil and lemon juice, helps to counteract the richness of the galette. It can be served either as a first or main course dish, depending on the size of the moulds used.

85 ml (3 fl oz, a small custard cup) moulds make 10 galettes

175 ml (6 fl oz , a large custard cup) moulds make 5 galettes

600 ml (1 pint, 2½ cups) mayonnaise

1 tablespoon tarragon, finely chopped

1 tablespoon Dijon mustard

2 cloves garlic, crushed

Salt and freshly ground black pepper

375 g (13 oz, ¾ lb) cooked beef, finely diced

5 teaspoons powdered gelatine

4 tablespoons beef stock

75 g (3 oz, a large bunch) mixed salad leaves

Green lentil dressing (p. 113)

Combine the mayonnaise, tarragon, mustard, garlic, seasoning and beef in a large bowl. Put the gelatine in a cup with the beef stock. Set in a saucepan containing about 2.5 cm (1 in) warm water and stir over a gentle heat until the gelatine is clear. Add to the mayonnaise and beef mixture. Stir to combine and divide between lightly oiled moulds. Chill until set.

To serve, turn out the moulds onto large individual plates, garnish with the mixed salad leaves and moistened with the green lentil dressing.

*F*ILLET OF BEEF WITH
ROASTED PEPPERS, AND MUSTARD
AND GREEN PEPPERCORN DRESSING

This is a simple but delicious salad of bitter leaves and roasted peppers, served with rare roast beef and accompanied by a mustard and green peppercorn dressing. It can be served as a first or main course dish.

SERVES 8

1 kg (2 lb) fillet of beef (beef tenderloin)

275 g (10 oz, 3½ large bunches) bitter salad leaves (such as sorrel, spinach, chicory or endive), cut into ribbons

2 red peppers, roasted and peeled

Mustard and green peppercorn dressing (p. 112)

Flat-leaved parsley

Tie the beef neatly at intervals and fry in a little butter and oil in a small roasting dish until brown on all sides. Transfer to a preheated oven at 200°C (400°F, gas mark 6) and cook for 30 minutes for rare beef. Leave to go cold, then slice thinly.

Pile the salad leaves to one side of 8 large plates. Arrange 3–4 slices of beef on each plate. Cut the peppers into large pieces and arrange on the salad leaves. Spoon a little of the mustard dressing over the edge of each piece of beef, garnish with flat-leaved parsley and serve immediately.

CHAPTER FOUR

DRESSINGS

A salad, either very simple or elaborate, is not complete without its light coat of dressing, whether it be a sharp mustard vinaigrette, a creamy mayonnaise or a simple sprinkling of fine olive oil and mature vinegar. The basis for all salad dressings is the oil and vinegar, and a large assortment of both are available. Some are soft and delicate in both taste and texture, such as the light olive oils and champagne vinegars, ideal companions for tender young leaves; others are sharper and more robust, like the aged red wine or sherry vinegars and heavier fruitier olive oils which complement the more substantial greens with their stronger taste and heavier leaf structure. The more powerful nut-flavoured oils and sweetened balsamic vinegars, however, require leaves of equal character and strength, such as the milder bitter endives, radicchio and other members of the chicory family. It is the skilful blending of all these elements that ensures that the texture and aroma of the salad is enhanced and its subtle flavours accentuated.

Oils, vinegars, herbs and
spices: the basic ingredients
of a salad dressing.

OILS

Oil is one of the most essential elements in a salad dressing, whether it be a vinaigrette or a mayonnaise. It is the underlying flavour on which the salad rests, and the wide variety of oils available makes it possible to choose one whose character will perfectly enhance the salad itself.

The word 'oil' comes from the Latin *olea*, and indeed olive oil has long been regarded as the finest oil for all culinary purposes, particularly that of salad dressings. Good-quality oil has a soft, rich and full-bodied aroma and flavour and, for me, is one of the most exquisite tastes in the world. It is this flavour, along with the oil's level of acidity, by which the quality of the oil is judged. The lower the level, the better the quality and the more aromatic the oil. Extra virgin olive oil, with only one per cent maximum acidity, is the finest quality olive oil.

The best oils are extracted from ripe or partially ripe olives from Italy, France, Spain and Greece. All quality oils are extracted from the olives under pressure, without the addition of water or chemicals. The first pressing after separating and filtering is the finest quality, referred to on labels as 'first cold pressed' or 'extra virgin oil'. Second-pressed oils have cold water added to the remaining pulp and are labelled 'fine' or 'extra fine' or sometimes 'virgin oil'. They have a slightly sharper flavour. A further pressing using hot water produces a third-grade oil with a strong coarse flavour referred to as 'pure' olive oil. The colour of olive oil ranges from pale golden yellow to a dark dense green. Next to olive oil, sunflower oil is one of the most versatile and widely used oils and, because of its pale colour and neutral taste, it lends itself well to blending with strong oils or using as a base for infusing herbs and spices. Other equally neutral oils are safflower, corn and rapeseed oil. In contrast, the nut oils have much more flavour with French walnut oil being the most luxurious. It has a rich topaz colour and a delicious nutty taste, which is not in the least overpowering. Hazelnut oil tends to be stronger and

A dressing and a salad should be the perfect marriage of complimentary ingredients. A mixed leaf and vegetable salad (p. 74), for example, is best simply dressed with a vinaigrette or citrus dressing (pp. 108–9).

combines well with sharp green leaves and mellow vinegars. The strongly flavoured oils such as soya bean and Chinese sesame seed oil, made from toasted sesame seeds, need to be diluted by blending with a more neutral oil, otherwise they are so distinctive and overpowering that they completely block out the delicate flavour of the salad ingredients. Light sesame oil, pressed from raw white seeds, is pale yellow in colour and pleasantly mild.

All salad oils should be sealed well after use and stored in a cool dark place. Nut oils are particularly delicate and tend to turn rancid in a few months, so they should be bought in small quantities and stored in the refrigerator.

Herb-flavoured oils can easily be made by combining 4 tablespoons of chopped herbs with 450 ml (15 fl oz, 2 cups) of olive oil or neutral flavoured oil or a combination of both in a sealed jar and leaving to infuse for about ten days, shaking occasionally. The oil is then strained into a bottle with a screwtop, a sprig of fresh herbs added and the bottle sealed. It will keep for two to three months.

VINEGARS

Most salad dressings are made from a base of oil plus an acid. This can be lemon or lime juice, yoghurt or soy sauce, but is more often vinegar – the liquid produced by the acid fermentation of an alcoholic liquid, most commonly red or white wine, but also cider, malt or rice, hence its French name *vin-aigre*, 'sour wine'.

As with the oils, there are several different types of vinegar, each with a different flavour, strength and quality. Some of the best are the wine vinegars from Orléans in the Loire region of France, the Balsamics from Modena in Italy, and the sherry vinegars from Spain.

Wine vinegar is produced from both red and white wines and, as a result, there are as many types as there are wines. The quality of the wine can also vary greatly but even the cheaper ones are preferable to the harshness of British malt vinegar. A good wine vinegar will resemble the wine it has been made from. Champagne vinegar is pale yellow and delicately flavoured. Red Rioja vinegar has a deep red colour and full fruity taste; if it has been aged in wood it will have a slightly smoky undertaste. Balsamic vinegar is a rich

reddish-brown vinegar from Italy, produced from a sweet wine and aged from four to over forty years. Even the young Balsamic vinegars have a sweet, spicy, nutty flavour. Sherry vinegar is a rich, sweet, aromatic vinegar from Jerez in Spain, made from the must used in sherry making and aged in wooden barrels. Cider vinegar, when good, has a gentle but distinct taste of apples, which makes it an excellent choice for salad dressings and for flavouring with herbs. Japanese white rice vinegar, made from rice wine, is pale yellow in colour with a slightly sweet flavour, prized for its smooth, clean and subtle taste. Brown rice vinegar, made from brown rice, is darker in colour and more pronounced in flavour. Chinese rice vinegar is usually sharper than the Japanese ones. Flavoured vinegars include those flavoured with ingredients such as garlic, peppercorns, chillies, herbs, spices, fruits and flower petals.

Fruit-flavoured vinegars: the quantity of fruit used to flavour the vinegar depends on the strength of flavour required and can range from 50 g (2 oz, ¼ cup) of fruit to 225 g (8 oz, 1 cup) per 450 ml (¾ pint, 1¾ cups) vinegar. Put the fruit in a preserving jar and crush to bruise and release the juices. Pour over white wine vinegar, cover and leave for several days on a warm sunny windowsill to infuse. Strain through a muslin-lined sieve. Bottle, seal and store in a cool dark cupboard.

VINAIGRETTE

Vinaigrette, or French dressing as it is often known, is the most widely used of all salad dressings and forms the basis of many others. It is a combination of oil and vinegar with the proportions varying from 1 part vinegar to 3 or more parts oil depending on the result required. Again, the type of oil and vinegar used depends on the type and style of dressing and the salad it is to dress.

TO MAKE 300 ml (10 fl oz, 1¼ cups)

250 ml (8 fl oz, 1 cup) olive or sunflower oil

or a combination of both

2–4 tablespoons wine vinegar

1–2 tablespoons salt

½ teaspoon freshly ground black pepper

I find the quickest and easiest way to make a vinaigrette is to combine all the ingredients in a screw-top jar and to shake vigorously until an emulsion is formed. This will give a quantity of dressing ready to hand for dressing salads over a period of days. Smaller quantities of dressings can be made directly in the salad bowl as required. Larger quantities of dressings can be made in a food processor; however, be careful not to overprocess or the result will be like mayonnaise.

Many additional ingredients can be added to this basic recipe in lesser or greater degrees depending on the strength and flavour of the vinaigrette required. It is very much a matter of personal taste and individual requirements, so be adventurous and experiment for yourself.

VARIATIONS

The following variations can be used with any single- or mixed-leaf salad, using the more robust dressings with the more substantial and flavoursome leaves.

MUSTARD VINAIGRETTE Add 2–4 tablespoons of Dijon or grain mustard or a combination of both to the basic recipe.

HERB VINAIGRETTE Add chopped, fresh herbs such as parsley, basil, tarragon, marjoram, chervil or mint to the basic vinaigrette.

CITRUS VINAIGRETTE Substitute the grated rind and juice of half a lemon, orange or grapefruit for the wine vinegar. Omit the mustard and add a pinch of sugar. Sunflower oil or part sunflower and olive oil makes a delicious, lighter dressing.

WALNUT OR HAZELNUT VINAIGRETTE Use 120 ml (4 fl oz, $\frac{1}{2}$ cup) sunflower oil and 120 ml (4 fl oz, $\frac{1}{2}$ cup) walnut or hazelnut oil with the rest of the ingredients.

CURRY VINAIGRETTE Add 1–2 teaspoons curry paste and 1–2 cloves garlic, crushed to the basic vinaigrette.

LIME VINAIGRETTE Substitute the grated rind and juice of 1 lime and 1 tablespoon sherry vinegar for the vinegar, and add 1 crushed garlic clove and $\frac{1}{4}$ teaspoon ground cardamom to the basic vinaigrette.

LIME AND POPPYSEED VINAIGRETTE Substitute the juice of 1 lime for the vinegar and add 2–4 tablespoons poppyseeds.

SPLIT CREAMY VINAIGRETTE Whisk in 50 ml (2 fl oz, $\frac{1}{4}$ cup) single cream to the basic vinaigrette.

GARLIC VINAIGRETTE Add 2–4 crushed garlic cloves to the basic vinaigrette.

HAZELNUT DRESSING

A rich, nutty dressing flavoured with Dijon mustard and freshly chopped chervil.

TO MAKE 85 ml (3 fl oz, $\frac{1}{3}$ cup)
1 small clove garlic, crushed
$\frac{1}{8}$ teaspoon Dijon mustard
4 tablespoons hazelnut oil
1 tablespoon white wine vinegar
Salt and freshly ground black pepper
1 teaspoon chervil, finely chopped

Combine the ingredients for the dressing in a small screw-top jar and shake vigorously to blend. Sprinkle over selected leaves and toss lightly to coat with the dressing. Serve immediately.

Walnut and Shallot Dressing

A richly flavoured nut dressing, perfect with a salad of robust greens.

TO MAKE 120 ml (4 fl oz, $\frac{1}{2}$ cup)

4 tablespoons sunflower or flavourless oil

1 teaspoon walnut oil

1 tablespoon sherry vinegar or red wine vinegar

Pinch salt and freshly ground black pepper

1 small shallot, very finely diced

Combine all the ingredients in a screw-top jar and shake well to emulsify. Serve with a salad of robust leaves.

Roquefort Dressing

This strongly flavoured dressing is best served with robust salad leaves or vegetables which will not be overpowered by its distinctive taste. Blue cheeses such as Stilton, Shropshire, Blue Cheshire or Danish Blue can be used.

TO MAKE 300 ml (10 fl oz, 1$\frac{1}{4}$ cups)

75 g (3 oz, $\frac{1}{4}$ lb) Roquefort, rinded and crumbled

1 tablespoon lemon juice

1 clove garlic, peeled and crushed

150 ml (5 fl oz, $\frac{2}{3}$ cup) natural yoghurt

6 tablespoons vinaigrette (p. 108)

2 tablespoons parsley, finely chopped

Combine all the ingredients in a food processor or liquidizer goblet and blend until smooth. Depending on the type of cheese used, it may be necessary to add a little extra natural yoghurt or vinaigrette to achieve the consistency of thin cream. Pour over the salad leaves or vegetables and toss gently. Serve immediately.

Mustard and Green Peppercorn Dressing

A rich, thick dressing that is more concentrated than the mustard vinaigrette (p. 109). Made from Dijon mustard and crushed green peppercorns, it is perfect with beef, chicken and bacon, strong cheese and robust vegetables or salad leaves.

TO MAKE 150 ml (5 fl oz, $\frac{2}{3}$ cup)

3 tablespoons green peppercorns, drained

2 tablespoons Dijon mustard

8 tablespoons sunflower oil

1 tablespoon white wine vinegar

2 teaspoons lemon juice

2 teaspoons warm water

Crush the green peppercorns in a pestle and mortar until roughly broken, stir in the Dijon mustard and gradually beat in the oil, adding a little at a time with the vinegar and lemon juice to form an emulsion. Stir in the warm water and store in a sealed jar.

Oriental Dressing

This is a variation on the basic vinaigrette, but more elaborate in its additions than the other variations. It is spicy, piquant and hot, and delicious with lightly cooked vegetables or bitter leaves.

TO MAKE 200 ml (7 fl oz, 1 cup)

120 ml (4 fl oz, $\frac{1}{2}$ cup) olive or sunflower oil

25 ml (1 fl oz, 1$\frac{1}{2}$ tablespoons) light sesame oil

3 tablespoons red wine vinegar

2 cloves garlic, peeled and crushed

3 tablespoons soy sauce

$\frac{1}{2}$ teaspoon tabasco sauce

$\frac{1}{2}$ teaspoon Szechuan pepper

$\frac{1}{4}$ teaspoon muscovado sugar

Combine all the ingredients in a screw-top jar and shake vigorously to form an emulsion.

Teriyaki Dressing

This hot, spicy dressing both piquant and hot, is excellent with sturdy vegetables and salad leaves, as well as poultry, meat and fish.

TO MAKE 200 ml (7 fl oz, 1 cup)

120 ml (4 fl oz, ½ cup) sunflower oil

25 ml (1 fl oz, 1½ tablespoons) light sesame oil

3 tablespoons red wine vinegar

2 cloves garlic, crushed

3 tablespoons Teriyaki sauce

½ teaspoon tabasco or chilli sauce

½ teaspoon Szechuan pepper

Pinch muscovado sugar

Combine all the ingredients in a screw-top jar and shake vigorously to form an emulsion.

Green Lentil Dressing

A wonderful, textured dressing with a sharp, nutty flavour. It is perfect for dressing a salad of robust leaves or rich meats.

TO MAKE 200 ml (7 fl oz, 1 cup)

25 g (1 oz, 3 tablespoons) whole green or yellow lentils

Boiling water

1 teaspoon lemon juice

3 tablespoons sunflower oil

Freshly ground black pepper

Bring a large saucepan of water to the boil and add the lentils, cook for 8–10 minutes until just tender but not mushy. Drain and refresh under cold running water until completely cold. Mix the lemon juice and oil together and stir in the lentils.

Chilli and Black Bean Dressing

A hot spicy dressing that is wonderful with a salad of robust greens.

TO MAKE 350 ml (12 fl oz, 1½ cups)

2 tablespoons sesame seeds

175 ml (6 fl oz, ¾ cup) water

1 tablespoon black bean sauce

1 tablespoon soy sauce

1½ tablespoons sweet chilli sauce

1 tablespoon light sesame oil

1 tablespoon chicken stock

1 tablespoon sherry or rice wine

1 tablespoon demerara (brown) sugar

1 tablespoon cider vinegar

1 tablespoon tomato purée

Fry the sesame seeds in a hot frying pan until lightly toasted. Add the water and stir in the rest of the ingredients. Bring to the boil, remove from the heat and leave to go cold. Add to 50 ml (2 fl oz, ¼ cup) non-scented oil like sunflower or safflower oil.

Champagne Dressing

A light, delicate dressing made from fine-quality olive oil and champagne vinegar.

TO MAKE 120 ml (4 fl oz, ½ cup)

1 small clove garlic, crushed

⅛ teaspoon Dijon mustard

6 tablespoons olive oil

1½ teaspoons white wine or champagne vinegar

Pinch salt

Freshly ground black pepper

Combine the ingredients for the dressing in a small screw-top jar and shake vigorously to form an emulsion; adjust the seasoning and sprinkle over the chosen salad leaves. Toss lightly to coat with the dressing and serve immediately.

TAPENADE

Tapenade is a rich purée of capers, olives and anchovies from Provence, which can be used in a great many ways. It can be served as a dip for crudités (p. 81), as a pâté to spread on crostini (p. 91), as a stuffing for hard-boiled eggs, or combined with vinaigrette and used as a dressing for salads and cold meats. This rich dark paste will keep for weeks in a sealed jar in the refrigerator and will certainly add spice and interest to a salad.

TO MAKE 250 ml (8 fl oz, 1 cup)

150 g (5 oz, 1 cup) black olives, stoned

1 × 50 g (1¾ oz) tin of anchovy fillets,
drained and rinsed

3 tablespoons capers, drained

50 g (2 oz, 3 tablespoons) tuna fish, drained

Juice of 1 small lemon

½ teaspoon Dijon mustard

25 ml (1 fl oz, 2½ tablespoons) olive or sunflower oil

Place the olives, anchovy fillets, capers, tuna fish, lemon juice and mustard in a liquidizer or food processor and blend until a very smooth paste has formed. Then still blending, very gradually add the oil, just as though you were making mayonnaise, until the mixture forms a thick paste. Taste and season with more lemon juice if necessary. Transfer to a screw-top bottle or jar and store in the refrigerator until required. To use as a salad dressing, add a little vinaigrette to a few tablespoons of tapenade to give a good flavour and a dressing consistency.

MAYONNAISE

Mayonnaise is a much more substantial salad dressing than vinaigrette or any of its variations. It, too, is an emulsion of oil and acid with the addition of egg yolks, which make it thick and smooth in texture. Extra virgin oil or a less highly flavoured oil or a combination of both can be used, depending on the taste required. Mayonnaise made with pure olive oil is very distinctive, rich and heavy and not to everyone's taste. For the best results, the eggs and oil should be at room temperature, the eggs beaten on their own for 1–2 minutes to thicken them slightly before the oil is gradually added. This will help prevent curdling. If the mixture does curdle, try adding a tablespoon of boiling water and beating hard. If this fails, start again in a clean bowl with a fresh yolk, adding the curdled mixture drop by drop until it is absorbed. I use an electric, free-standing or hand-held mixer for making mayonnaise.

TO MAKE 300 ml (10 fl oz, 1¼ cups)

2 egg yolks

¼ teaspoon English mustard powder

300 ml (10 fl oz, 1¼ cups) olive or sunflower oil

1–2 tablespoons lemon juice or wine vinegar

A pinch of powdered white pepper

¼ teaspoon salt

Put the yolks and mustard in a medium-size bowl and beat for ½–1 minute with an electric whisk until pale and thick. Then add the oil, drop by drop, beating continually, until about half the oil has been added. Now the oil can be added in a steady stream, still beating continually. When all the oil has been added and the mixture is very thick, add the lemon juice or vinegar and seasoning. If the mayonnaise is too thick, stir in a little warm water to bring it to the correct consistency. Transfer to a bowl or jar, cover carefully to prevent a skin from forming and store in the refrigerator. Homemade mayonnaise should be kept in the refrigerator and only for a few days.

VARIATIONS

FOOD PROCESSOR MAYONNAISE This is a very quick and easy way to make mayonnaise and gives an excellent silky-smooth result, which is less thick and lighter in texture. Substitute a whole egg for one of the yolks and blend with the mustard. Then add the oil in a thin stream while still blending. When the mixture begins to thicken, scrape the sides of the bowl, add the lemon juice or vinegar and season to taste.

GARLIC MAYONNAISE Add 3 cloves of crushed or pounded garlic to the finished mayonnaise.

MUSTARD MAYONNAISE Stir 1–2 tablespoons coarse grain, Dijon or green peppercorn mustard into 300 ml (10 fl oz, 1¼ cups) mayonnaise.

HERB MAYONNAISE Stir 1 teaspoon each of finely chopped tarragon, parsley, chervil and chives into the prepared mayonnaise.

CURRIED MAYONNAISE Gradually add the 300 ml (10 fl oz, 1¼ cups) prepared mayonnaise to ½–1 tablespoon of curry paste.

BASIL MAYONNAISE Add 6 tablespoons finely chopped basil leaves to 300 ml (10 fl oz, 1¼ cups) mayonnaise.

LEMON MAYONNAISE Substitute the juice of 1 lemon for the vinegar in the basic mayonnaise and add the grated rind of half the lemon.

Aïoli

Although this famous and well-loved French Provençal sauce is basically a strongly flavoured garlic mayonnaise, it is really much more. For aïoli, the garlic is pounded to a very smooth paste in a pestle and mortar before beating in the yolks and then incorporating the oil. It is not just simply adding crushed garlic to mayonnaise, although that itself will produce a perfectly well-flavoured dressing.

Aïoli is traditionally served with raw or cooked vegetables such as carrots, French beans, sweet red peppers, hard-boiled eggs or boiled fish, generally salt cod, or cold meats. It is a delicious sauce and well worth the effort – if you like garlic!

SERVES 4

TO MAKE 300 ml (10 fl oz, 1¼ cups)

5 cloves garlic

2 egg yolks

300 ml (10 fl oz, 1¼ cups) olive oil

½ tablespoon lemon juice

Pinch salt

Peel the garlic cloves and pound to a smooth paste in a pestle and mortar or work in a bowl using the end of a rolling pin. I generally crush the cloves in a garlic press to begin with.

Unless the mortar is very large, transfer the garlic to a bowl, add the egg yolks and continue to beat with the pestle or a hand-held electric mixer (although this method would be frowned upon by the purists, it is much quicker and easier). The traditional method is unrealistically time consuming and a food processor is unsuitable as it causes the garlic to develop a bitter taste. When the garlic and yolks are well blended, begin adding the oil, just as for mayonnaise, drop by drop until the sauce begins to thicken and about half the oil has been added. Continue to add the oil in a thin stream, beating all the time as the mayonnaise thickens. If it becomes too thick, add a few drops of the lemon juice and continue like this until the oil and lemon juice are both incorporated. According to Elizabeth David, a good aïoli should be practically solid. Add the salt to season. Do not add the salt at the beginning of the mixing as this may cause the mayonnaise to remain thin or separate and curdle. Pile into a small bowl and serve with whatever vegetables, fish or cold meats are available.

BIBLIOGRAPHY

Campbell, Susan, *Cottesbrooke, an English Kitchen Garden*, Century Hutchinson, London 1987

Connery, Clare, *Quick and Easy Salads*, BBC Books, London 1992

Dowell, Philip and Bailey, Adrian, *The Book of Ingredients*, Michael Joseph, London 1980

Hamilton, Geoff, *Successful Organic Gardening*, Dorling Kindersley, London 1987

Holt, Geraldine, *Geraldine Holt's Complete Book of Herbs*, Conran Octopus, London 1991

Jordan, Michael, *Mushroom Magic*, Elm Tree Books, London 1989

Kenton, Leslie and Susannah, *Raw Energy*, Century, London 1984

Larkcom, Joy, *The Salad Garden*, Frances Lincoln, London 1984

Leggatt, Jenny, *Cooking with Flowers*, Century Hutchinson, London 1987

Loewenfeld, Claire and Back, Philippa, *The Complete Book of Herbs and Spices*, David and Charles, Newton Abbot 1974

Phillips, Roger, *Wild Food*, Pan, London 1983

The Reader's Digest Association, *Food from your Garden*, London 1977

The Royal Horticultural Society, Gardeners' Calendar, Consultant Editor John Main, Macdonald Orbis, London & Sydney 1987

INDEX

Numbers in italics refer to illustration captions

ACKNOWLEDGEMENTS

I am deeply indebted to Michael Dover, my publisher at Weidenfeld and Nicolson, for inviting me to write a book on salads. It was his enthusiasm that inspired the book and enabled me to convey my passion for all things fresh and leafy in words and photographs.

To Coralie Hepburn, my longsuffering editor, my thanks are also due for her patience and encouragement, and to my friend and photographer Christopher Hill, without whose splendid pictures the book would have been much less colourful and the project less enjoyable.

Many other colleagues and friends also enabled me to write *The Salad Book*, encouraging and educating me with their own extensive knowledge, and sharing so generously not only their talents but also their time and magnificent gardens. In particular I am most grateful to botanist Barbara Pilcher and plant and gardening authority Rosemary Verey, whose influence over the years and whose help on this book have gone some little way to making a gardener out of a cook.

I am also indebted to the Royal Horticultural Society for permission to photograph their model herb and vegetable gardens at Wisley.

In my search for knowledge I have also turned to many authors for information and advice. The bibliography provides a full list but I would especially like to thank Joy Larkcom, Geoff Hamilton, Roger Phillips and Geraldine Holt whose books I have referred to frequently and whose work I much admire.

I am also grateful to Albert Forsythe, antique dealer and friend, for so graciously providing his showroom and pieces from his collection for many of the photographs and for his patience throughout all the days of disruption. Thanks also to Kay Gilbert of Equinox in Belfast for providing much of the very fine china, glass and cutlery which helped make my salads look so beautiful, and to Philip Devlin, specialist supplier of fruit and vegetables to the catering trade in Northern Ireland, for selecting my salad leaves and vegetables with such care.

Last, but not least, my thanks to Doreen McBrien, my ever faithful secretary and an enthusiastic gardener, without whose help my life would be much more complicated and much less orderly.

Photographs © Weidenfeld & Nicolson Ltd 1993

First published in Great Britain in 1993 by
George Weidenfeld & Nicolson Limited
Orion House, 5 Upper St Martin's Lane
London WC2H 9EA

British Library Cataloguing in Publication Data
A catalogue for this book is available from the
British Library.

ISBN 0-297-83208-5

Designer: Harry Green
House Editor: Coralie Hepburn
Sub-Editor: Frances Cleary

Typeset by Keyspools Ltd, Golborne, Lancs
Printed and bound in Italy